COCKTAILS
and
CONSOLES

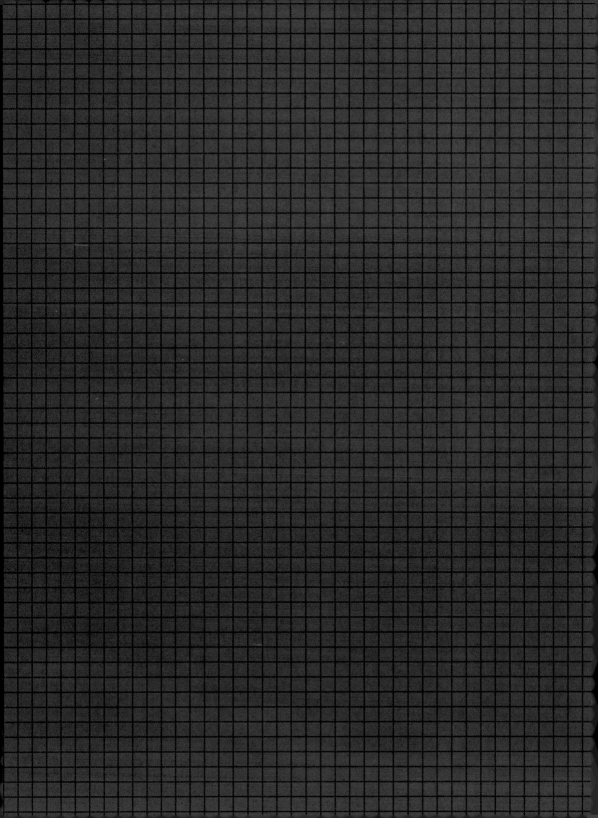

COCKTAILS
and
CONSOLES

75 VIDEO GAME—INSPIRED DRINKS TO LEVEL UP YOUR GAME NIGHT

Elias Eells

Illustrated by Solji Lee

RUNNING PRESS

PHILADELPHIA

Running Press
Hachette Book Group
1290 Avenue of the Americas, New York, NY 10104
www.runningpress.com
@Running_Press

First Edition: September 2024

Published by Running Press, an imprint of Hachette Book Group, Inc. The Running Press name and logo are trademarks of Hachette Book Group, Inc.

The Hachette Speakers Bureau provides a wide range of authors for speaking events. To find out more, go to www.hachettespeakersbureau.com or email HachetteSpeakers@hbgusa.com.

Running Press books may be purchased in bulk for business, educational, or promotional use. For more information, please contact your local bookseller or the Hachette Book Group Special Markets Department at Special.Markets@hbgusa.com.

The publisher is not responsible for websites (or their content) that are not owned by the publisher.

Print book cover and interior design by Tanvi Baghele

Library of Congress Cataloging-in-Publication Data
Names: Eells, Elias, author. | Lee, Solji, illustrator.
Title: Cocktails and consoles : 75 video game-inspired drinks to level up your game night / Elias Eells ; illustrated by Solji Lee.
Description: First edition. | Philadelphia : Running Press, 2024. | Includes index.
Identifiers: LCCN 2023044285 (print) | LCCN 2023044286 (ebook) | ISBN 9780762486915 (hardcover) | ISBN 9780762486922 (ebook)
Subjects: LCSH: Cocktails. | Video games. | Cocktail parties. | LCGFT: Cookbooks.
Classification: LCC TX951 .E356 2024 (print) | LCC TX951 (ebook) | DDC 641.87/4– dc23/eng/20231205
LC record available at https://lccn.loc.gov/2023044285
LC ebook record available at https://lccn.loc.gov/2023044286

ISBNs: 978-0-7624-8691-5 (hardcover), 978-0-7624-8692-2 (ebook)

Printed in China

APS

10   9   8   7   6   5   4   3   2   1

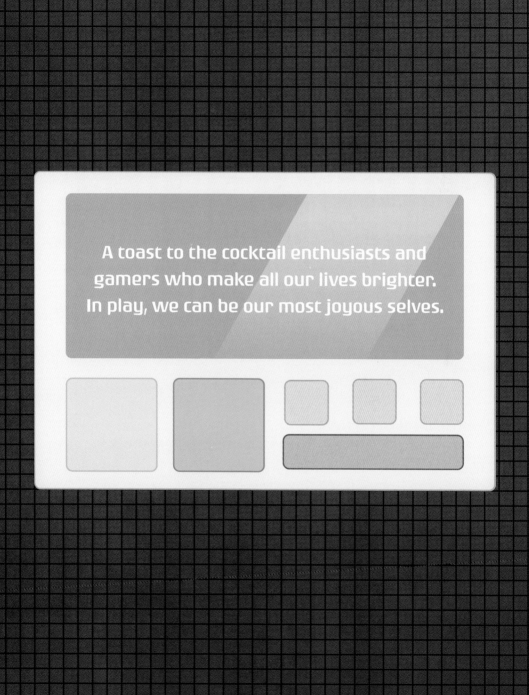

A toast to the cocktail enthusiasts and gamers who make all our lives brighter. In play, we can be our most joyous selves.

CONTENTS

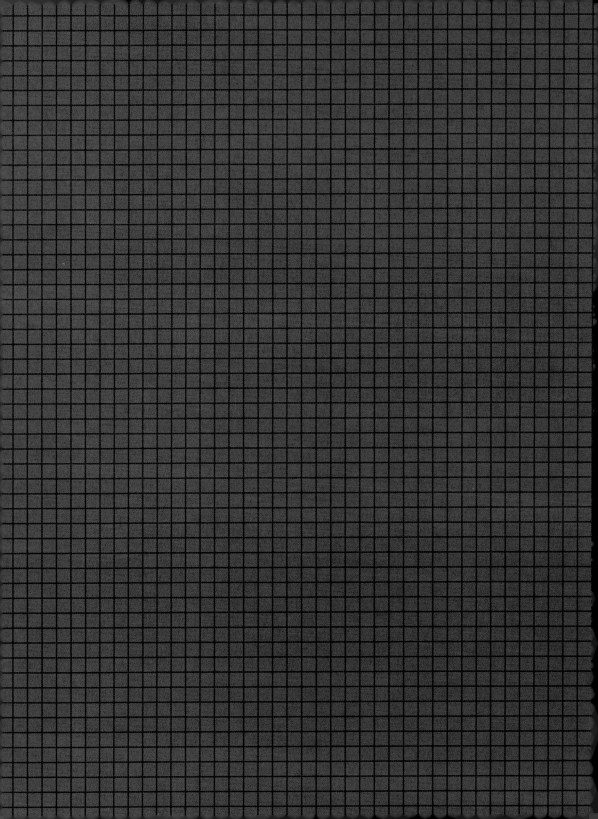

THE TUTORIAL

We drink cocktails to celebrate our wins, to unwind at the end of a long day, to bring a little something special to our weekend gaming sesh. We drink mocktails because we want to have our wits about us when we're crushing those combos or solving an especially devilish puzzle. Great drinks are for gamers of all skill levels and inclinations.

This book contains a survey of the wide world of gaming, with iconic characters, landmark titles, and sleeper favorites. Our cocktails and mocktails are stirred, shaken, blended, and set, because there are as many types of cocktail enthusiasts as there are gaming fanatics. Plus, a few bonus snacks and munchables will make your next co-op cocktail party a smash!

Start your evening with a refreshing Sardegna Simulator Spritz (page 151) and munch on the Loot Box Bridge Mix (page 157) as you battle it out in the arena. A Noble Pursuit (page 90) or Flood Shot (page 137) will offer a long treat and a quick sip. A smoky-sweet Wildfire Wood (page 81) is the perfect digestif. Round out the evening with A Sweet Reward! (page 73) and a couple Astral Cookies (page 48).

However you game and however you drink, you'll find something fun, fresh, and filling between these pages!

PRESS START!

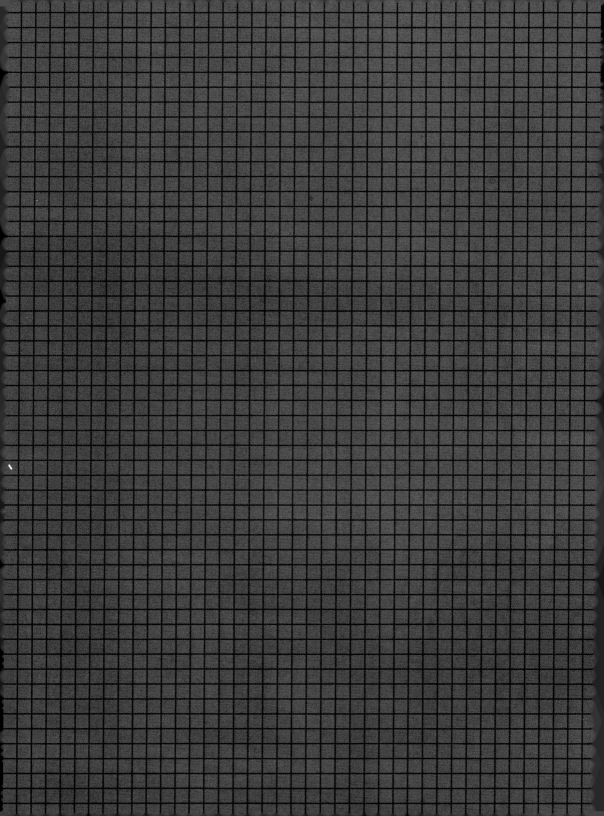

TOOLS OF THE TRADE

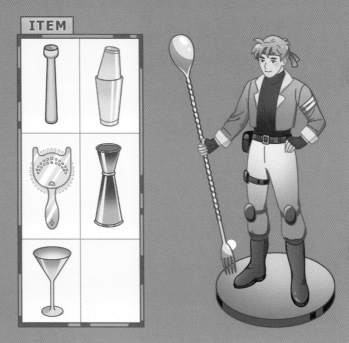

ITEM

When you're equipping your character in an RPG, you want to have the right items—weapon, shield, helmet, gloves, boots, and amulets—everything you need to venture out into the wilderness and battle the forces of darkness. Prepping your bar cart is much the same. There are drinks for different playstyles (shaking versus stirring) and tools to match. Make sure that you're ready for adventure by having the essential tools at your disposal.

There are four tools you need to make 90 percent of all the cocktails and mocktails in the world. These tools are totally standard and universal—no need to worry about porting! With a jigger, a shaker, a spoon, and a Hawthorne strainer in hand, you'll be able to make all the drinks in this book without a worry.

Jigger

Consistent cocktails begin with the proper measuring tool. I recommend a Japanese-style jigger with interior measurements. The tall, narrow shape of the Japanese-style jigger makes it easier to consistently pour with ease. The standard measurements in most cocktails and mocktails are ¼ ounce, ½ ounce, ¾ ounce, 1 ounce, 1½ ounces, and 2 ounces. The best jigger will have all of these measurements, but if your jigger is missing the ¼-ounce measurement, you can still add ¼ ounce of an ingredient to your drink with a simple trick: if there's another ingredient that you need ½ or ¾ ounce of, you can then top off your jigger over that ingredient to the next measurement line, which will give you ¼ ounce.

BAR BYTES

Just as many games are Japanese imports, when the art of craft cocktails was on the decline in the US in the 1980s and '90s, the tools of the trade were being preserved and perfected in Japan. A rich cocktail culture focused on high-precision techniques and rigorous discipline for beautiful service.

Cocktail Shaker

I recommend a two-piece Boston shaker rather than a three-piece cobbler shaker. While a three-piece cobbler shaker looks elegant on a bar cart, it is less functional than a Boston shaker. Because the metal surfaces are in constant contact along the rim of the tins, as the drink chills, the metal contracts, and a solid seal can become a vacuum seal, trapping your drink until you can fight and twist it open. Then, with several stout taps and mighty twists, you'll finally open your shaker, only to find that a few years of those struggles have warped the metal and left the cobbler shaker prone to leaks. Besides, the large holes of the cobbler's built-in strainer allow more and larger ice chips to end up in your glass when you strain and serve the drink. Trust me, stick with a two-piece shaker; it'll make your life easier and keep the focus on your favorite games.

The two-piece Boston shaker should always have a big 28-ounce tin. For the small tin, you have the option of 18-ounce stainless steel or 16-ounce heat-treated glass. Do not use your favorite pint glass for shaking cocktails, as the thermal shock can cause the glass to break—and then you've not only missed out on a drink but also ruined a favorite glass. The heat-treated glass is traditional and useful for stirring cocktails because it both allows you to keep an eye on your ice as it melts and offers a quieter stir. That said, my recommendation is for tin on tin; it's more beginner-friendly because it seals more easily and, more importantly, *unseals* more easily. Two flexible pieces of metal moving against each other make for a much smoother process than one flexible metal and one rigid glass. Equip the tool build that feels right for your mixing style!

HOW TO USE A BOSTON SHAKER

Build your cocktail in the small tin. You build in the small tin to ensure that you don't fill the shaker with too much liquid and risk an imperfect seal. Traditional wisdom cautions to start with your cheapest ingredient and work your way up to the most expensive, in case of spilling, but there's no wrong way to build a cocktail in the shaker.

Add your ice last. Ice will immediately start melting and diluting your drink, so you don't want to do it earlier and risk being distracted. Nothing is sadder than a watery cocktail.

Cap the small tin with the big tin with one side flush against the metal. A stout tap with the flat of your hand should seal the deal.

Shake over your shoulder with the small tin facing behind you. If your shaker isn't perfectly sealed, the last thing you want to do is spill some of your drink on a friend or teammate. Shake until chilled and the metal is frosted.

Open the tin with a stout tap. Use the flat of your hand to firmly tap the exposed side of the shaker, causing the metal to flex and unseal.

Strain your drink. Place your Hawthorne strainer on top of the big tin, over the liquid, and pour decisively into your cocktail glass.

Enjoy your frosty fresh cocktail or mocktail!

Bar Spoon

The chef's knife of the bar world, the bar spoon is a versatile tool whose utility goes well beyond simple stirring. The ideal bar spoon has a droplet weight at the end and a tight coil. You can use the coil to steady your stir and to pour a liquid, like seltzer or ginger beer, down to the bottom of your glass. You can also measure with your bar spoon. Sometimes you want just a touch of some delicate or assertive ingredient, and fortunately, most bar spoons hold about ⅛ ounce. We'll see how that can be useful when adding a whisper of a flavor rather than a full-throated shout in many of our recipes.

When stirring with your bar spoon, keep the back of the spoon against the wall of your shaker tin or mixing glass. Hold the barrel of the spoon between your index and middle fingers and stir. It can feel like doing the worm with your fingers, and practice makes perfect.

Hawthorne Strainer

If you have only one strainer, this should be The One. Equally suited to shaken or stirred cocktails and mocktails, the Hawthorne strainer is equipped with several small holes and a tight coil to catch ice chips. It will allow the finished cocktail or mocktail to strain into your glass while keeping any ice or muddled fruit pulp in the shaker.

Some of our recipes may call for a conical strainer for dual-wielding . . . I mean double-straining . . . but for most cocktail and mocktail preparations, the Hawthorne strainer is the only tool in its class you'll need.

Bonus Tools

Muddler
The muddler is an iconic bar tool, and one that you'll often think you need, but I bet you'll find that you muddle far less often than you expected. It's nice to have to express fresh flavors from fruit, herbs, and berries, but it's definitely a less common technique than your standard shake and stir. Look for a muddler with a flat bottom, as toothed muddlers will tear up whatever ingredient you're trying to muddle and express bitter compounds, while making a bigger mess.

Conical Strainer
If you want to ensure that every last chip of ice or fleck of muddled herb stays out of your cocktail glass, you'll want to double-strain them, running the liquid through both the coil of your Hawthorne strainer and the fine mesh of a conical strainer. Dessert drinks and fizzes are the most commonly double-strained cocktails and mocktails. The fine-mesh strainer is also a useful tool for straining off citrus peels or nut meal when making syrups and cordials, but you can use a funnel and cheesecloth if you prefer.

Elbow Juicer
You can juice your citrus any way you like, with an electric juicer, a reamer, or your hand, but the easiest and cleanest way to juice citrus is with an elbow-style juicer. Simply cut your fruit in half crosswise, place one half in the juicer dome side up, and squeeze. You can juice directly into your jigger, but the wider target of a measuring cup makes it easier to avoid a sticky countertop.

Mixing Glass
It is possible to stir cocktails in your shaker, but a pitcher-style mixing glass looks great on a bar cart and makes stirred drinks a breeze. Look for one in the 750 mL range; it's nice to be able to stir up two or three cocktails at the same time when you're entertaining guests.

Twist Peeler
You can cut your garnishes, citrus twists, and swaths with a paring knife or vegetable peeler, but it is nice to have a dedicated tool for those thin twists. Look for a sharp blade and cut your twist by rotating the fruit rather than turning the knife.

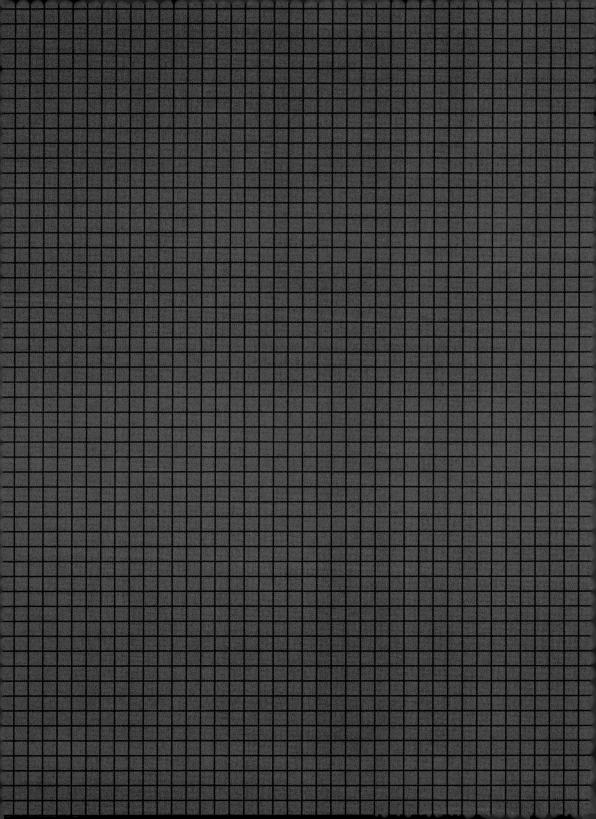

GLASSWARE

If the bar tools are the weapons of your bar cart, glassware is the armor class. There is technically no *wrong* way to serve a drink, but the ways that drinks are served and the style of glass is more than an aesthetic choice. The proper glass is designed to augment and enhance the experience of sipping your cocktail or mocktail. After all, you could make it through the lava demon boss in your ice-resistant armor, but it wouldn't feel quite right, would it?

Stemmed Glassware

Stemmed glassware is for drinks served "up": chilled and without ice. Why? You want your drink to stay cold, and a stemmed glass allows you to hold the stem without warming the bowl of the glass in the palm of your hand. The classic V-shaped martini glass is recognizable but not so user-friendly when sipping, so picking a coupe or Nick and Nora glass will have your cocktail or mocktail safe in hand and frosty cold.

Old-Fashioned/Rocks Glasses

These glasses are for drinks served "down": chilled and with ice. The glass will warm in your hand as you sip your drink, encouraging the ice to melt and diluting a strong (in alcohol or flavor) drink over the course of your sipping. If you play a lot of games with high focus and intermittent breaks, a slow-burn stirred drink you can linger over is definitely the drink for you. Whether served with a single large ice cube or a whole glass of crushed ice, the old-fashioned glass is comfortable in the hand and perfect to keep by your side as you game without any fear of spilling.

Highballs

Highball glasses are designed for drinks that are "long," which means they have an increased volume from soda, sparkling wine, or the highly structured foam of a fizz. Bubbly and refreshing, these drinks are perfect for warm weather and slow sipping. Both cocktails and mocktails work well in this format, like when you want to keep your wits about you playing a game or when you're chilling after an exciting PvP matchup.

The swizzle glass and hurricane glass are also highball glasses, but they are used for swizzled or blended drinks made with crushed ice, which adds lots of volume to your drink—and dilutes it quickly.

Large-Format Drinking Vessels

The pitcher and the punch bowl are essential for party hosting! You don't want to spend all evening making individual drinks for your friends and loved ones; better to get a big batch made before the party starts and spend the afternoon or evening visiting with your guests and playing your favorite games.

It is often easy to find good punch bowls at secondhand shops and estate sales. Keep your eyes peeled for high volume and a great deal.

BAR BYTES: PREPPING FOR A PARTY

You'll use more ice at a party than you think, so make sure to plan ahead. It's always best to use good dense ice (made in an ice tray) for cocktails, and you can always bank several batches in the days ahead of the party if you have the freezer space. If you're using your fridge's ice maker or bagged ice, bear in mind that is going to be less dense than ice made in an ice tray and will melt faster and break apart more easily. If you're using fridge ice or bagged ice, shake your cocktails a little less because they will dilute faster.

Snacks are a must! Whether you're serving cocktails, mocktails, or a mix of both, it's no fun gaming on an empty stomach. Save your mood and please your guests with an array of small bites and tasty treats. Offer something salty to wet your whistle, and something sweet to celebrate your victories.

COMPONENTS:
SPIRITS AND OTHER INGREDIENTS

Building up your bar can be a daunting task. There are lots of specialty ingredients used in cocktails and mocktails and it can be hard to know where to start. Fortunately, many ingredients have a long shelf life, so that bottle of bitters is never going to go bad—trust me, I've tried 100-year-old bitters and they were still delicious! Even syrups and vermouth will last several weeks to several months. But it can be hard to know what ingredients you'll need or use the most of when planning a co-op party or just looking for something to pair with your next gaming sesh. What I recommend is picking one or two drinks that sound good and getting the ingredients for those; then, as you want to try new things, add on as you go.

Starting with a base spirit like gin or rum is a safe bet because it will appear in a lot of recipes, both the original ones in this book as well as many classic cocktails. Another quick cheat code is to keep your focus on categories of ingredients rather than specific brands. There are no cocktail judges: if the drink tastes good to you, then you made it right! If you need to make substitutions, go for it, and we'll have some advice on how to do that along the way.

This book is set up so that every ingredient will be used for at least two drinks. That way you won't have to buy something that gets used only once. Or, if you find *the* drink that you want to make and enjoy for a whole season, then you'll have enough on hand to do so without needing to press pause on your game to run to the store. I know that happens with me and games; sometimes all you want to do is start a new farm in *Stardew Valley*, mix up some Stardrop Swizzles (page 85), and relax with them all summer long!

The Bases

Brandy

A distilled spirit made from fruit, primarily grapes, brandy is warming and approachable. A subtle fruitiness pervades even very dry brandies and brings an old-world charm to cocktails. Some brandies are specific to the region of production, like cognac, made in the Cognac region of France. Others are labeled generically. Both grape and apple brandies appear in this book. I recommend Pierre Ferrand, Laird's, Copper & Kings, and St. George.

Used in: Civ Fizz (page 35), Life Apple (page 53), The Cake Is a Lie (page 72), Ashfire Mead (page 94), Lady Boyle's Last Party Punch (page 122), Timefall Fizz (page 131), B. J. Blazkowicz (page 134), Plasmid (page 140)

Gin

Gin is a distilled spirit flavored primarily with juniper. This versatile cocktail ingredient comes in a number of different styles, from the juniper-forward London dry to the more citrusy American style. Other gins or gin cousins, like genever, are malty with a complex depth to their flavor. Find a gin you like or several to try out and explore how your cocktails change depending on the gin you use. I recommend Hayman's, Tanqueray, and Bols Genever for recipes in this book.

Used in: Zero Suit Spritz (page 43), The Miles Edgeworth MarTEAni (page 56), A Morning in Martinaise (page 62), Garden Party (page 79), Exoplanet (page 98), Blood and Sans (page 101), Wizard Blizzard (page 109), Lady Dimitrescu Fizz (page 143), Refillable Potion (page 153)

Rum

A distilled spirit made from sugarcane, rum is a common base for both shaken and stirred drinks. While rum is used in a lot of tropical and fruity drinks, that is not the only space for rum on the bar cart, and dessert drinks can make use of the complex chocolate and caramel notes in a top-quality rum, for example. Rum sees a wide variety of stylistic expressions, from the clean brown sugar notes of an aged rum to the sugarcane grassiness of Brazilian cachaça. I recommend Cruzan, Novo Fogo, and Privateer.

Used in: Barge of Death (page 51), Grassy Gruel (page 52), KoMaiTaiDa (page 60), Sirrus and Achenar (page 69), A Sweet Reward! (page 73), Stardrop Swizzle (page 85), Noble Pursuit (page 90), Mass Relay (page 100), Finishing Move (page 148), Impostor Shot (page 163), The Hook (page 164)

Tequila

A distilled spirit made from agave, tequila is assertive and exciting, lending a distinctive flair to any cocktail where it is used. My house tequila is Lunazul—a clean, neutral tequila that offers a nice versatility in mixed drinks.

Used in: Mariogarita (page 40), The Fragrance of Dark Coffee (page 57)

Vodka

Vodka can be distilled from most anything, from fruit to grain and more. The spirit is distilled and filtered to remove rogue flavor compounds and leave the focus on neutral ethanol. Because the goal of producing a vodka is to eliminate flavor, vodka often takes the backseat in cocktails, but that simply allows the other flavors to shine. Vodka plays well with others, the perfect support.

Used in: Ring Drop (page 44), Tetrimino Jell-O Shots (page 66), The Lich King (page 108), Wizard Blizzard (page 109), The Ghost (page 112), Liquid Snake (page 116), High-Octane Highball (page 120), James Bond's Martini (page 135)

Whiskey

A distilled spirit made from grain, whiskey (spelled "whisky" if it's from anywhere besides the United States or Ireland) has dozens of expressions across the world and many of those styles are available in most liquor stores. From spicy, grain-forward rye to mellow sippin' bourbon to sharp, smoky Scotch, there is a whiskey for every occasion. My favorite brands include Woodford Reserve, Jefferson's, Old Overholt, Ardbeg, Cutty Sark, and Jameson.

Used in: Oregon Trail Buck (page 29), Colossal Cave Julep (page 31), The Shores of Hell (page 37), Bourbon Slush (page 63), Wildfire Wood (page 81), Water of Rebirth (page 102), Miriel, Pastor of Vows (page 105), Lady Boyle's Last Party Punch (page 122), The Spectacular Spider-Sour (page 126), SurRYEvor (page 128), B. J. Blazkowicz (page 134), Bravo Spritz (page 138), Button Smash (page 147), Hanzo Highball (page 152), Falcon Punch (page 162), The Hook (page 164)

Sparkling Wine

Sparkling wine lends an effervescent fizz to many cocktails, both for individual drinks and punches. Whether you choose champagne, prosecco, cava, or any other sparkling wine, it will have some effect on the final taste of your cocktail, but there are no wrong choices. Look for a mid-range bottle, between $10 and $25.

Used in: Zero Suit Spritz (page 43), Barge of Death (page 51), Sirrus and Achenar (page 69), Garden Party (page 79), Agent 47 (page 119), Lady Boyle's Last Party Punch (page 122)

Absinthe, Aperitifs, and Amari

Bittersweet liqueurs and herbal concoctions are the real specialty components in the world of mixology. They bring complex flavors to cocktails that can't be replicated with home infusions and level up libations to the highest quality. Many amari and aperitifs are specific to one brand, such as Campari. My favorite absinthes are St. George Absinthe Verte and Copper & Kings Absinthe Blanche.

Absinthe used in: Ice-9 (page 59), Flood Shot (page 137)

Aperitifs used in: Mariogarita (page 40), Bravo Spritz (page 138), Plasmid (page 140)

Tea

A useful ingredient in cocktails, but especially in mocktails, a strongly brewed tea will not only bring its signature flavor, but also stand in for the bitterness or bite of alcohol. Tea can add an accent flavor in alcoholic drinks as well. The recipes in this book use several varieties of black tea, green tea, and a few herbal spice teas.

I recommend using an English breakfast blend when looking for an ordinary black tea base, but there is a wide range of flavor profiles to work with. For example, Earl Grey, a black tea blended with bergamot, plays well with citrus bitters and can add a gentle citrus peel bitterness to cocktails and mocktails. Lapsang souchong, a Chinese black tea, is smoked and can be used to add that umami depth to both cocktails and mocktails. It also works well as a nonalcoholic base for mocktails but will appear most often in this book as a syrup to bring smoky warmth to cocktails.

Used in: Porcelain and Peppermint (page 47), Pom of Power (page 49), Bourbon Slush (page 63), Hershel Layton's Top Hat (page 70), Berry and Mint Burst (page 103), Ether (page 111), Lady Boyle's Last Party Punch (page 122), Refillable Potion (page 153)

The Modifiers

Liqueurs

A liqueur is an alcoholic ingredient composed of a base spirit and other flavorings, including a sweetener. There are a wide range of liqueurs that bring a kaleidoscope of flavors to cocktails. Herbal liqueurs like crème de menthe or crème de violette, citrus liqueurs like curaçao, and nutty liqueurs like amaretto all add their distinctive notes to our drinks. There is such a variety of flavors in the world of liqueurs that it is easy to find a good brand in the desired flavor category.

Vermouth

An aromatized fortified wine, vermouth is an essential ingredient in many classic cocktails. Because it is lower ABV (alcohol by volume) than spirits, vermouth should be refrigerated after opening and used within a month of opening. A half bottle, 375 mL, is often the best choice when purchasing vermouth, unless you are planning a party and intend to use more. I recommend Dolin for dry vermouth and Carpano Antica Formula for sweet vermouth.

Bitters

The spice rack of the bar, bitters are typically measured in dashes, not ounces. Some bitters come in dropper bottles and, as a general rule, 1 dropperful is roughly equivalent to a solid dash. A little goes a long way, and it is easy to add more but hard to add less. If you want to taste your bitters on their own, try a few dashes in some sparkling water, or splash a drop on the back of your hand and taste them neat.

When shopping for bitters, there are most likely some options available at your local liquor store. You can also purchase directly from many bitters manufacturers online. Here is a short list of a range of bitters based on the classic flavor families.

Aromatic: Angostura, The Bitter Housewife Cardamom, Strongwater or Fee Brothers Black Walnut

Citrus: Regans' Orange (austere, dry, and complex), Fee Brothers West Indian Orange (sweeter and more approachable), Scrappy's Grapefruit

Citrus

Citrus juice, whether lemon, lime, grapefruit, or orange, is a key component of classic cocktails because the sourness brightens drinks. Citrus drinks will be shaken with ice, rather than stirred, for aeration and lighter body. Shaken sours should be bright and bracing, not soft and supple.

Freshly squeezed juice is always the best choice for brightness of flavor and complexity, though keep in mind that many flavor compounds in citrus fruits begin to dull and fade within hours of juicing. If you are using a bottled juice, I recommend Santa Cruz organic juices because they are not from concentrate and retain as much of the freshly squeezed brightness as any bottled citrus juice is able to.

Sweeteners

Sweeteners come in a range of flavors, from the uncomplicated sweetness of Simple Syrup (page 17) to the vinegar tang of a shrub (page 20) or the nutty floral complexity of Orgeat (page 23). The sweetener is often one of the distinctive flavors in a cocktail or mocktail: after all, there are only so many base spirits and different types of citruses.

Sweeteners add more than sweetness and flavor to a drink, they also add texture. Often the sweeteners are the densest ingredients in a cocktail or mocktail and contribute to the mouthfeel of a drink. If something tastes a little thin, try adding a bar spoon of simple syrup and see how the drink changes.

Cream

A key component of dessert cocktails, heavy cream adds texture and depth to a cocktail, while softening more assertive flavors. Dairy drinks should be shaken, not stirred, for extra froth and foam.

BAR BYTES: BATCHING COCKTAILS

Batching and bottling your stirred cocktails is a great way to prep for a party. You don't want to spend all evening mixing up a fresh drink for your guests when you could be gaming instead—you deserve to have a good time at the party, too. Some drinks scale up well, especially stirred cocktails like Ashfire Mead (page 94), and others can be readily converted to punches. Others, particularly dairy-based and dessert drinks like the V-Buck (page 156), should not be batched because they will curdle or separate in the bottle or the punch bowl, and no one wants that! Here's an easy way to scale up different kinds of cocktails and mocktails:

1 serving	7 servings	20 servings
1 ounce	1 cup	1 750 mL bottle (3 cups)
¾ ounce	¾ cup	500 mL (2 cups)
½ ounce	½ cup	375 mL (1½ cups)
¼ ounce	¼ cup	250 mL (1 cup)

But . . . we now have a new problem: When you stir up an individual cocktail, you're doing more than cooling and blending the liquid, you're diluting it as well. That's what takes the typical 3 ounces of liquid to the 4½ ounces or so that you'll strain into your cocktail glass. To bottle a stirred drink, you should also add ⅓ to ½ part water to your batch before bottling. Also note that with bitters, a little can go a long way and you will not need to add 20 dashes to your bottled cocktail. You can choose to either add your bitters when you serve each portion of the drink or stick to a good 6 to 8 dashes (approximately what you would use for 2 drinks). With bitters, it's easy to add more but hard to add less, so taste as you go and adjust to suit your palate. The character creation system for this batched drink is so robust!

Shaken drinks made with citrus don't bottle as well as stirred cocktails, but they make fantastic punch for a party! Mix up a large batch of the cocktail a few hours before your party, saving any fizzy components for when it's time to serve. You want your citrus to stay fresh and still have time to do the rest of your preparation. When it's time to get the party started, add several large ice cubes to your punch bowl along with your batched drink and let the melting ice do the dilution for you.

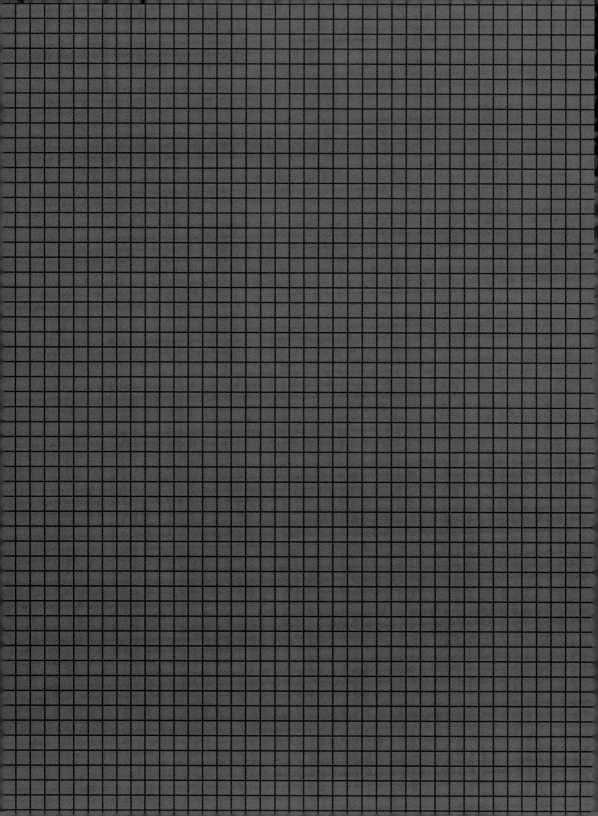

BUFFS: SYRUPS, CORDIALS, AND SHRUBS

Simple Syrup

It doesn't get any easier than simple syrup! A neutral sugar like granulated will give you the clearest, cleanest-tasting simple syrup. Others, like demerara or natural cane sugar, will have a more caramelized flavor and a richer, muddier color. Modify to suit your tastes!

SKILL LEVEL: 1
YIELD: 1½ CUPS

1 cup sugar

1 cup water

Cold Method: Combine the sugar and water in a resealable bottle and shake to mix. It's as easy as that!

Hot Method: Combine the sugar and water in a small saucepan and simmer on the stovetop, stirring until dissolved. Bottle and allow to cool before using.

HOT TIP:

Label your syrups! It's easy to forget what's in each bottle, and the smell test can only go so far. Make sure you know what ingredient is in each bottle and how long it has been in your fridge.

BAR BYTES: SIMPLE SYRUP VERSUS RICH SIMPLE SYRUP

Sugar and simple syrup do more than sweeten a drink, they also add texture and mouthfeel. A rich simple syrup is even more intense than regular simple syrup, so it's good for a punch or when you want to add just a bit of sweetness and a lot of depth to your cocktail. To make a rich simple syrup, use 2 cups sugar and 1 cup water.

Simple Syrup Variations

The simple syrup format is endlessly versatile. It's almost like crafting different types of armor, except you do see the results. Think of your simple syrup variations as elemental armor—this one has fire resistance, this one has poison resistance—all useful tools in your arsenal to be deployed in the appropriate time and fashion.

For tea syrup: Mix 1 cup strongly brewed tea with 1 cup sugar, then shake.

For red wine syrup: Mix 1 cup dry red wine with 1 cup sugar, then shake.

For honey syrup: Mix 1 cup warm water with 2 cups honey, then shake.

For oat syrup: Mix 1 cup Oatmeal Brose (page 19) with 1 cup sugar, then shake.

For herbal syrup: Add fresh herbs like mint to your simple syrup mixture so that they are completely submerged. Store in the fridge overnight and taste-test the simple syrup in the morning. For more intensity of flavor, replace with another batch of fresh herbs and taste again the next day. Be wary of over-extracting from one batch of herbs, as that will release tannins and lead to a bitter syrup instead of being fresh and bright.

For cinnamon syrup: Add 1½ cinnamon sticks to your simple syrup mixture, using the hot method. Store in the fridge and strain after 24 hours.

Oatmeal Brose

Oatmeal brose is the water left over from making overnight oats.

SKILL LEVEL: 1

YIELD: 2 CUPS

3 cups water

1 cup rolled oats

¼ teaspoon salt

Bring the water to a boil in a small saucepan over medium heat, then add the oats and salt. Stir to combine. Remove from the heat after 5 minutes, cover, and let cool overnight. Strain off the liquid using a conical strainer or cheesecloth.

Bonus: Warm up the oats with a little brown sugar for a tasty breakfast.

Grenadine

Traditionally made with pomegranate juice, this fruit syrup can also be made with a variety of fruit juices, like cherry or blueberry, for an interesting variation on the classic preparation.

SKILL LEVEL: 2

YIELD: 3 CUPS

2 cups pomegranate juice

2 cups sugar

¼ teaspoon rose water

¼ teaspoon orange blossom water

1 tablespoon brandy (as a preservative)

Pour the pomegranate juice into a small saucepan set over medium heat, then add the sugar. Stir until the sugar is dissolved. Pour ¾ cup of the mixture into a measuring cup and set it aside. Heat the remaining mixture in the saucepan until it is reduced by half, about 15 minutes. Once the grenadine is reduced, add the reserved ¾ cup. Remove from the heat and stir in the rose water and orange blossom water. Add the brandy, then bottle your grenadine. Store in the fridge and use within 2 months.

For variations: With cherry, I omit the orange blossom water, and with blueberry, I omit the rose water.

Peach Shrub

Shrubs are fruit syrups made with vinegar. They are bright and tangy, perfect for adding a refreshing bite to cocktails and mocktails alike. It is best to make this shrub in the summer when peaches are at their prime, but it can be used year-round for a sweet bit of summertime.

SKILL LEVEL: 2
YIELD: 2½ CUPS

6 peaches, peeled, pitted, and cut into ½-inch chunks (about 4 cups)

1½ cups sugar

1 teaspoon salt

1½ cups apple cider vinegar

Combine the peaches, sugar, and salt in a jar and stir to combine. Cover and let sit at room temperature for 3 to 6 hours, then refrigerate overnight, stirring occasionally to help dissolve the sugar. After 24 hours, add the vinegar, cover, and return the jar to the fridge for at least 24 hours or up to 72. Strain the mixture and bottle. Store in the fridge and use within 6 months.

Melon Shrub

This lightly green shrub is a refreshing summer sipper with clean melon flavor and a pleasant zing.

SKILL LEVEL: 2
YIELD: 2½ CUPS

1 small honeydew melon, peeled, seeded, and cut into ½-inch chunks (about 3 cups)

2 cups sugar

1 teaspoon salt

1½ cups white vinegar

Combine the melon, sugar, and salt in a small saucepan and gently simmer over medium heat for 10 minutes to soften the melon. Transfer the mixture to a jar and stir to combine. Cover and let sit at room temperature for 3 to 6 hours, then refrigerate overnight, stirring occasionally to help dissolve the sugar. After 24 hours, add the vinegar, cover, and return the jar to the fridge for at least 24 hours or up to 72. Strain the mixture and bottle. Store in the fridge and use within 6 months.

Ginger Syrup

Fiery fresh ginger brings a rich herbal heat to cocktails and mocktails alike.

SKILL LEVEL: 2
YIELD: 2 CUPS

1 (4-inch) piece ginger, cut into ½-inch pieces (about ½ cup)

1 cup water

1⅓ cups sugar

1 tablespoon vodka (as preservative)

Combine the ginger and water in a blender and blend until smooth. Add the sugar and stir to combine. Transfer to a jar, cover, and refrigerate overnight. After 24 hours, strain off any remaining ginger particles with a conical strainer. Add the vodka and bottle. Store in the fridge and use within 3 months.

Variation: For a softer, sweeter ginger syrup, use ginger in the hot method of making a simple syrup, just as you would with cinnamon (see page 18).

Raspberry Liqueur

There are commercially available berry liqueurs, like Chambord, but nothing compares to the fresh zing and fruity brightness of homemade. Plus, this technique allows you to control the sweetness of your batch!

SKILL LEVEL: 2
YIELD: 4 CUPS

1 (10-ounce) package fresh or frozen raspberries

1⅓ cups sugar

1 (750 mL) bottle vodka

Combine the raspberries, sugar, and vodka in a jar and stir to combine. Cover and store in a cool, dark place for at least 2 weeks, stirring occasionally to help dissolve the sugar. Taste and adjust the sweetness as necessary. If you want more berry brightness, strain off the old berries and replace with fresh. When the liqueur tastes right to you, strain the mixture and bottle. The liqueur will not go bad, but the flavor will be freshest and brightest if used within 1 year.

Hot Chili Tincture

Here's a unique way to add a bite to your cocktails! Changing your peppers will shape the flavor and spiciness of each batch: jalapeños offer a greener, more vegetal heat than cayenne peppers or the sharp burn of a habanero. Don't forget your gloves with this one!

SKILL LEVEL: 3
YIELD: 2 CUPS

1⅓ cups fresh hot peppers of choice

2 cups vodka

Wash the peppers and pat dry with a paper towel. Remove the stems and slice the peppers down the middle lengthwise. You may discard or preserve the seeds, depending on how hot you want your tincture to be—the more seeds, the hotter it will be. Put the peppers in a jar and add the vodka. Cover and let sit in a cool, dark place for up to 2 weeks, stirring every other day. Strain off the peppers and then bottle. Enjoy your fiery mixture indefinitely.

Orgeat

This is *the* best cocktail syrup of all time. Everybody loves orgeat, and it's a sure way to give your cocktails and mocktails a nutty, floral sweetness. Making orgeat can be a bit time consuming, so it is best to make a large batch, but it is well worth the effort.

SKILL LEVEL: 3

YIELD: 5 CUPS

4 cups almonds

3 cups water

3½ cups sugar

¼ cup brandy

1 teaspoon orange blossom water

Pulse the almonds in a blender or food processor until you have a rough meal. Set aside.

Combine the water and sugar in a large saucepan and bring to a boil. Boil for 5 minutes, stirring periodically. Remove the pan from the heat and mix in the almond meal. Stir to combine. Return the mixture to the stovetop and simmer over medium-low heat for 5 minutes. Remove from the heat and transfer to a jar. Once it's cooled slightly, cover and refrigerate for at least 8 hours or up to 24. Strain off the almond meal with a fine-mesh strainer. Stir in the brandy and orange blossom water, bottle the orgeat, and store in the fridge. Use within 3 months and remember to shake before using.

Citrus Cordial

A citrus cordial is a great method for preserving the complex flavor of citrus—from lemons and limes to oranges, grapefruits, and more. It melds the brightness of fresh juice with the depth of zest and peel for an exciting way to enhance your cocktails and mocktails with something that you already have on hand. Making a citrus cordial can have slight variations, depending on the size of the fruit being used, but don't worry! Each batch is unique, so focus on the proportions and it will be delicious every time.

SKILL LEVEL: 3

YIELD: 3 CUPS

4 or 5 larger fruits (oranges, grapefruits) or 10 to 15 smaller fruits (lemons, limes), well scrubbed

2 cups sugar

⅓ cup vodka (as preservative)

Put the citrus fruits in a large saucepan, cover with water, and gently simmer over medium-low heat for 10 minutes—warm citrus expresses more oils and juice. Remove the fruit and pat dry with a towel, then zest; you should get about 1½ cups. Put the zest in a jar, cover with 1⅔ cups of the sugar, and let sit at room temperature for 3 hours, stirring every 45 minutes to create an oleo-saccharum, a sugar oil. Next, juice the fruits; you should get about 2 cups. Add the juice and remaining ⅓ cup sugar to the jar, cover, and refrigerate for 24 hours, stirring occasionally. Strain off the citrus peel and stir in the vodka. Bottle and store in the fridge. Use within 3 months, and be sure to shake before using.

Buying Syrups

Want to level up your cocktail skills before making syrups? In a pinch and don't have time to craft these delicious concoctions? Don't worry, you can buy them! Simple, orgeat, passion fruit, ginger, and more—there are a number of commercial syrup options that will save you a headache in the kitchen. Check out Yes Cocktail Co. and Small Hand Foods, which both produce excellent orgeat and passion fruit syrup, or Pratt Standard, which makes the best ginger syrup I've ever tasted—with exactly the right balance of sweetness and fiery ginger heat. Element Shrubs offers a variety of flavors, and their peach tamarind or honeydew jalapeño make good substitutes for the homemade shrubs used in this book.

PIXELATED ELIXIRS

A classic is a classic for a reason. This chapter looks back on some iconic gaming titles of yesteryear. The origins of popular genres and the expansive range of playstyles are apparent from the arcade days to early PC favorites. Traditional games with traditional cocktails and mocktails, these are foundational favorites.

Pong

A classic's classic, this game demonstrates the simple elegance that video games can offer. Introduced as an arcade game in 1971 and for home consoles in 1975, *Pong* helped bring video games beyond the arcade and made them a staple of home entertainment. A two-dimensional simulation of table tennis, it was an enormous success and one of the most significant games ever released. *Pong* was inspired by an electronic Ping-Pong game included on the Magnavox Odyssey, the first home video game console, which was originally created as a training exercise for Atari computer engineer Allan Alcorn. His version of virtual table tennis was such high quality that the game was manufactured and published—and history was made. Magnavox sued for patent infringement in 1974 and the suit was settled out of court, but the Atari version stood the test of time and continues to charm half a century later.

Pong Punch

You need a partner to play *Pong,* so we need enough to go around for Player 2—or a whole party! A throwback to the bright citrus flavors and cosmic vibes of the '70s, this mocktail will keep your wits sharp and your party guests lively all evening long.

YIELD: 8 MOCKTAILS

1 (32-ounce) can pineapple juice

1½ cups water

¾ cup Tang

1 (2 L) bottle ginger ale

1 orange, sliced, for garnish

Mix the pineapple juice, water, and Tang in a large pitcher with several large ice cubes to keep cool. (Large ice cubes melt slowly, and you don't want your punch to dilute too quickly.) Top with the ginger ale and garnish with the orange slices. Serve in highball glasses.

The Oregon Trail

"You have died of dysentery." When *The Oregon Trail* premiered in 1971, little did we know how evocative and enduring that phrase would be, but fifty-plus years later, this game is as iconic as ever. While the original text-based version of the game appeared in 1971, the graphics of the 1985 release for the Apple II computer would define the series. Set in 1848, players follow a wagon train of settlers from Independence, Missouri, to the Willamette Valley in Oregon. The dangers are many and the journey is fraught. You'll need to make good use of your supplies, take care when fording rivers, and guard against the random acts of cruel fate. Can you make it out west?

Oregon Trail Buck

One of the classic minigames in *The Oregon Trail* is game hunting—you need food to survive as you make your way west, and an elk is a fine prize. They only appear on the western portion of the trail, so you've already made it a good way to your destination and definitely deserve a cocktail and a rest. A take on the traditional cocktail, this buck is bright and bittersweet, with a triple citrus twist and a gentle honey kiss.

YIELD: 1 COCKTAIL

2 ounces rye whiskey

¾ ounce lime cordial (see page 24)

¾ ounce fresh lemon juice

½ ounce honey syrup (see page 18)

6 to 8 dashes aromatic bitters

4 to 6 dashes orange bitters

1 (12-ounce) bottle ginger beer

Combine the rye, lime cordial, lemon juice, honey syrup, and bitters in a shaker, then add ice. Shake until chilled and frosty, then strain into a highball glass over fresh ice. Top with the ginger beer and enjoy a refreshing highball along the trail.

BAR BYTES: BITTERS AND PATENT MEDICINES

Looking at a bottle of bitters, it's easy to remember that they're an old-fashioned favorite. The heavy text and mismatched paper of the Angostura aromatic bitters call to mind the patent medicines of the nineteenth century, some of which would have been used on the Oregon Trail. And this is a deliberate choice on the part of bitters manufacturers. Bitters, the spice rack of the bar, are herbal concoctions used to accent and refine your cocktails and mocktails. They have two broad families, aromatic and citrus, both of which are used in the Oregon Trail Buck. Aromatic bitters, like Angostura, are the most familiar for cocktail connoisseurs, with baking spice notes like cinnamon, clove, and allspice. Citrus bitters feature the brightness of orange, lemon, lime, or grapefruit, along with the bitter depth of the citrus peel.

Bitters were medicines once upon a time, but now they've made a much happier home on the bar cart. Gentian, the primary bittering agent in many bitters, is a natural digestive aid, leading to the common folk hangover remedy of bitters and soda. For more information on the history of bitters as medicine, check out Camper English's *Doctors and Distillers*.

Colossal Cave Adventure

One of the original computer games, *Colossal Cave Adventure* is a landmark title and classic text-based game. An early prototype of both the visual novel and the adventure game formats, it's modeled on the experiences of creator and designer William Crowther's exploration of Mammoth Cave in south-central Kentucky. While the 1975 game draws on real caves and caving expertise, it is not wholly realistic fiction, and includes fantasy elements like dragons and magic spells, which were introduced by developer Don Woods when the game was expanded in 1977. The fingerprints of *Colossal Cave Adventure* are all over many popular genres of video game, from the roguelike to the action-adventure, and the dungeon crawl aspects will be immediately familiar to many gamers. For modern fans, a 3D remake called *Colossal Cave* was released in 2023, a new avenue for connecting the history of the genre with contemporary consoles. For the historian and connoisseur, *Colossal Cave Adventure* is an essential title.

Colossal Cave Julep

Kentucky is home to both the largest cave system in the world and the world's most robust spirits tourism industry, the Bourbon Trail, making it the perfect place to draw inspiration from. Mellow bourbon, herbal mint, and earthy dark chocolate meet in this riff on the classic mint julep, one of the oldest styles of cocktail for one of the oldest classic games. It's good in late spring but great in autumn as the weather starts to chill. In the cool dark of a cave, it's nice to have a frosted glass and refreshing cocktail.

YIELD: 1 COCKTAIL

2 ounces bourbon whiskey

½ ounce mint simple syrup (see page 18)

½ ounce dark crème de cacao

2 dashes aromatic bitters

1 mint sprig, for garnish

Fill a julep cup or old-fashioned glass with crushed ice. Pour the bourbon, mint syrup, and crème de cacao over the ice, add the bitters, and stir to mix. Top with fresh crushed ice and garnish with the mint sprig.

Pac-Man

This is the arcade game's arcade game. Introduced in 1980, the game places the player in control of the iconic bright yellow Pac-Man as he traverses a maze, eating as many power pellets and fruit as he can while avoiding the ghosts Blinky, Pinky, Inky, and Clyde. The game was a runaway success that spawned sequels and decades of merchandise, establishing Pac-Man as one of the most recognizable characters in the history of video games.

Pac-Man Punch

Dots and ghosts are not all the wonders to be found in Pac-Man's labyrinth. Bonus points come from consuming the cherries, strawberries, oranges, apples, and melons scattered about. It's those flavors that inspire this mocktail punch. While there's no lime in *Pac-Man*, it helps to brighten the punch, and grapes were introduced in 1982's *Pac-Man Plus*, a sequel that was nearly identical to the original game. This is a perfect refreshing fruit punch for a summer afternoon of gaming with friends.

YIELD: 20 MOCKTAILS

1 (750 mL) bottle sparkling apple cider

3 cups fresh orange juice

2 cups white grape juice

1½ cups fresh lime juice

1 cup Melon Shrub (page 20)

½ cup cherry grenadine (see page 19)

½ cup fresh strawberries, sliced, for garnish

½ cup pitted cherries, for garnish

Combine the cider, fruit juices, shrub, and grenadine in a punch bowl. Add a large ice ball (see box on page 154) and several fruit-infused ice cubes (see box). Stir to combine, then garnish with the strawberries and cherries.

+1 Alcohol: Add 2 cups white rum and increase the cherry grenadine to ¾ cup for a drink with a little bite.

Garnish Game: Fruit-Infused Ice Cubes

You'll need a large ice tray for this project, suitable for 2-inch ice cubes. If you want your fruit to be entirely encased in ice, start by filling the cells of your ice tray one-third of the way with water and freezing. Take the ice tray out of the freezer and add a fresh strawberry or pitted cherry to each cell of the ice tray, then fill the rest of the way with water. Freeze and add to your punch for a slow dilution with extra fruit flavor.

For an easier option, you can just add the strawberries and cherries when you fill the ice tray with water, but the cubes will have a bare edge on the bottom where the fruit sank.

Tapper

An arcade classic, *Tapper* puts the player behind the bar as a harried bartender tasked with fulfilling the orders of his thirsty customers. Collect tips and avoid spilling beer or breaking a mug as you progress through four themed levels. The game is delightfully challenging, so the first level in a Western-style saloon is the most recognizable, but advancing toward the sports bar, punk rock club, or space station will move your score closer and closer to the world record of 3,162,125 set by Gregory Erway in 2005.

Bartop Float

The game was originally branded by Anheuser-Busch, but in 1984, to avoid the suggestion that they were marketing alcohol to minors, the game was rethemed with root beer instead. It was this nonalcoholic version that was shipped to arcades around the world and inspired this mocktail.

YIELD: 1 MOCKTAIL

1 (12-ounce) can root beer

¼ ounce lapsang souchong syrup (see "tea syrup" on page 18)

1 scoop vanilla ice cream

2 to 4 dashes aromatic bitters

Pour the root beer into a chilled pint glass, then add the tea syrup and ice cream. Stir to combine and top with the bitters. Save the sliding for in the game, you don't want to spill your drink.

Civilization

The landmark series of turn-based strategy games follows competing civilizations from the Stone Age to the Space Age. Whether through cultural dominance or conquest, the goal remains the same: improve, survive, and thrive. Drawn from historical civilizations and celebrating notable figures, each culture offers unique bonuses and individual paths to victory or defeat. A defining series in the 4X strategy genre, *Civilization* continues to drive players to eXplore, eXpand, eXploit, and eXterminate their rivals.

Civ Fizz

Through subjugation or through sophistication, the goal of *Civilization* remains the same: universal dominance. This bright fizz effervesces and engages, with an elegant foam that towers like a space elevator. The perfect fizz takes strategy, patience, and practice, ideal for an evening of raising your favorite civilization to total victory.

YIELD: 1 COCKTAIL

1½ ounces cognac

¾ ounce fresh lemon juice

½ ounce Raspberry Liqueur (page 22)

¼ ounce Ginger Syrup (page 21)

1 bar spoon rich simple syrup (see box on page 18)

1 large egg white (see box on page 143)

Seltzer

Combine the cognac, lemon juice, raspberry liqueur, ginger syrup, simple syrup, and egg white in a shaker. Shake for 15 seconds without ice. Add two ice cubes and shake until melted and the drink is chilled. Double-strain into a highball glass and top with seltzer.

BAR BYTES: THE DRY SHAKE

The dry shake, without ice, is the key to a tall foam in a fizz. By shaking your drink without ice, you aerate the cocktail and whip the egg. The reverse dry shake (see box on page 73) is easier but results in a softer, more supple foam. For a truly architectural masterpiece, a skyscraper of a fizz, you want the initial dry shake. Give it a try!

DOOM

The game that pioneered the first-person shooter (FPS) genre, *DOOM* follows an unnamed space marine, Doomguy, as he battles his way through the moons of Mars. Originally released for MS-DOS in 1993, gameplay is the focus, with a simple plot delivered in short messages between episodes: fight your way through the stages toward the exit. There are hazards from monsters, environmental dangers like radioactive waste or crumbling architecture, and locked doors that require finding a key or trigger switch. If *DOOM* seems de rigueur now, it is only because it is an essential title for speedrunners and fans of video game history and classic battling FPS adventures.

The Shores of Hell

The second episode in *DOOM*, "The Shores of Hell," sees Doomguy move through the research facilities of the Martian moon Deimos, confronted with sinister architecture and demonic invaders. The forces of Hell have taken the chrome and steel of the space facility and left it rugged, transformed into wood and stone, organic and aggressive. A gateway to Hell beckons—and with it the need for a cocktail that is rich and red, with a fiery heat. The only way out is through.

YIELD: 1 COCKTAIL

2¼ ounces rye whiskey

½ ounce cherry grenadine (see page 19)

¼ ounce Ginger Syrup (page 21)

2 to 4 dashes Peychaud's bitters

1 bar spoon Hot Chili Tincture (page 22)

1 flaming orange wheel (see box), for garnish

Combine the rye, grenadine, ginger syrup, bitters, and chili tincture in a mixing glass, then add ice. Stir for 20 seconds, then strain into an old-fashioned glass over a single large ice cube. Garnish with the flaming orange wheel.

Garnish Game: Flaming Orange Wheel

Wash 2 oranges and slice into wheels. Put the wheels in a jar and add 1½ cups overproof rum and 1 cup sugar, making sure the oranges are completely covered. Cover and soak overnight at room temperature.

When it is time to garnish your drink, use tongs to remove an orange wheel and place it on the rim of the glass. Use a long match to ignite and enjoy.

Note: The orange wheels can be stored indefinitely in this mixture but may become softer with age. Keep at room temperature; the warmer the base temperature of the alcohol, the easier it is to ignite.

PLATFORMERS AND METROIDVANIAS

Moving your character through uneven terrain, leaping and jumping through obstacles, exploring a new environment crawling with foes—that's the name of the game with a platformer. Traditionally linear and with a focus on gameplay over story, when you bring in more action-adventure elements you find the Metroidvania, with new areas to explore and new tools in your inventory. These games will keep you on your virtual toes as you bob, weave, and maneuver through every challenge.

Super Mario Bros.

"It's-a-me, Mario!" Perhaps no single video game character is more recognizable than the red-capped Italian plumber who hops, skips, and jumps his way to the rescue of the darling Princess Peach. From his debut in 1981 to dozens of games across multiple genres, spinoffs for his green-hatted brother Luigi, and two feature films, for a short king, Mario looms large over the world of gaming. First seen as the original player character for the arcade game *Donkey Kong*, he would go on to have his own arcade feature in 1983's *Mario Bros.* That was a mere prelude to greatness, and the diminutive plumber really came into his own with 1985's *Super Mario Bros.*, the first 2D side-scrolling platformer in the franchise. Over the next forty years, Mario and his cohort have explored platform worlds in both 2D and 3D and as well as open-world adventures, go-kart racing, puzzle games, and party games. After decades of popularity, the whimsy remains, and Mario is beloved by gamers of all ages.

Mariogarita

Inspired by the Mushroom Kingdom's finest plumber, this iconic hero deserves a frosty margarita with a bright red Italian twist after a long day of collecting coins, punching blocks, and saving Princess Peach.

YIELD: 1 COCKTAIL

1 ounce tequila

1 ounce fresh lime juice

¾ ounce Campari

½ ounce blood orange liqueur

Combine all the ingredients in a shaker, then add ice. Shake for 15 seconds, then pour into an old-fashioned glass.

Garnish Game: Rimming a Glass

If you wish to rim the edge of your Mariogarita glass with salt, you can try to dampen the edge of the glass with the rind of a freshly juiced lime, but I prefer a simpler approach. I use a damp paper towel to lightly wet the edge of my glass, then roll the rim of the glass in a small dish (a saucer or salad plate will do the job) filled with a good amount of flaky kosher salt. Use more salt than you think you'll need as that will help ensure an even coating. Kosher salt is the salt of choice, as the flakiness makes it easier to adhere to the rim of the glass. When you're satisfied with the amount of salt on the rim of your glass, set it aside and mix up the rest of your cocktail.

Metroid

This is the series that created an entire subgenre of action-adventure platforming games. The original *Metroid* debuted in 1986 as the bounty hunter Samus Aran battles Space Pirates in pursuit of the titular Metroids, parasitic organisms with the potential to be used as biological weapons. With each new region of the game explored, new power-ups, abilities, and challenges emerge, hallmarks of the Metroidvania subgenre. With more than a dozen games in the series and even more planned, *Metroid* has been a hallmark of the 2D and 3D platformer genre for nearly forty years. The game and the series are notable not only for the pioneering impact, but also for being an early game for speedrunners and for showcasing a female protagonist in Samus Aran, who inspired our Metroid drink.

Zero Suit Spritz

Synonymous with the series is Samus Aran's red-gold space suit with a glowing visor, known as the Power Suit. That is until 2004, when she first wears her blue-gray Zero Suit in the game *Metroid: Zero Mission*. Now the look is almost as iconic as the Power Suit, and it's the outfit that she wears in *Super Smash Bros. Brawl* as one of the eight original, or "perfect attendance," characters in the series. Taking a cue from this bounty hunter's calm, cool demeanor and iconic jumpsuit, this spritz is a complex herbal refresher perfect for coming down from the heat of battle or a summer afternoon.

YIELD: 1 COCKTAIL

1 ounce London dry gin

½ ounce green chartreuse

¼ ounce crème de violette

¼ ounce blue curaçao

2 ounces sparkling wine

2 ounces tonic water

1 orange peel, for garnish

Combine the gin, chartreuse, crème de violette, and curaçao in a large wineglass with ice. Stir to combine, then top with the sparkling wine and tonic water. Garnish with an expressed orange peel (see box).

Garnish Game: Expressing Citrus Peel

The oils of a citrus peel add fresh aromatic notes when garnishing a cocktail or mocktail. Pinching the peel to express those oils adds an elegant finishing touch to your drink. Use a peeler to cut a wide swath of your chosen citrus. Take the peel and hold it lengthwise over the surface of your glass. Pinch to express the oil—you'll see a small mist on the surface of the drink. You can smell and taste the difference. Try it and see!

Sonic the Hedgehog

Debuting in 1991, *Sonic the Hedgehog* was a platformer with simple mechanics, a great story, and a truly distinctive hero. The first game sold more than 24 million copies and is regarded as one of the greatest games of all time. The character and the different worlds that he races through battling the evil Dr. Eggman and his lackeys have appeared in more than seventy games, showing the enduring legacy of the franchise and the endless innovation of the Sega team. Always fresh and a favorite for three decades, *Sonic* just goes to show that a classic is a classic for a reason.

Ring Drop

Whether you're racing through the Green Hill Zone or hunting down Chaos Emeralds, you need a good drink in hand. Nothing gets you into the Hydrocity Zone like a refreshing cocktail, and you need those gold rings if you're gonna win the game. A quintessential '90s game needs a quintessential '90s drink, so sip on this Day-Glo blue vodka sour that's tart, bright, and beautifully garnished. Gotta go fast!

YIELD: 1 COCKTAIL

2 ounces vodka

¾ ounce fresh lemon juice

½ ounce blue curaçao

¼ ounce Simple Syrup (page 17)

1 three-ring lemon twist (see box), for garnish

Combine the vodka, lemon juice, curaçao, and simple syrup in a shaker, followed by ice, then shake it up. *Fast.* Shake for 15 seconds, then strain into a stemmed cocktail glass. Garnish with a three-ring lemon twist.

Garnish Game: Three-Ring Twist

Take a lemon and a twist peeler or paring knife. Hold the two ends of the lemon between your thumb and forefinger. Cut into the lemon with the twist peeler and rotate the fruit away from you, cutting into the peel and working your way around the lemon. Cut three short twists with this method. Twist the lemon peels into rings, and pin them along a cocktail skewer, holding the two ends together. Save the lemon for fresh juice in your cocktails and mocktails.

Temple Run

An endless running game with the aesthetics of an ancient jungle civilization that would do Indiana Jones or *Tomb Raider* proud, *Temple Run* is one of the most recognizable and popular mobile games of the 2010s. Choosing from a range of player characters with different strengths and weaknesses, you are fleeing through a Mesoamerican temple with a troop of demonic monkeys desperate to reclaim the golden idol of the temple, hot on your heels. The game has no end until you run into an obstacle, fall into the water, or are overtaken by the temple guardians. How long can you last?

Shirley Temple Run

The Shirley Temple is the best-known mocktail there is and, if you're of a certain generation, you've probably had your share of them. The original Shirley Temple is a blend of grenadine and ginger ale, a stalwart of the early twentieth century exploration that is evoked in this dynamic game. For our version, we have added passion fruit because it is one of those magical ingredients, like a treasure in a lost temple, that makes everything you put it in taste tropical. With this refreshing mocktail, you'll be ready to race through the jungle and happy to share with your friends!

YIELD: 1 MOCKTAIL

1 ounce passion fruit syrup

½ ounce Grenadine (page 19)

1 (12-ounce) can ginger ale

Pour the passion fruit syrup and grenadine into a highball glass with ice. Top with the ginger ale and stir to mix. Garnish with a tropical umbrella.

Cuphead

Introduced in 2017, *Cuphead* is a run-and-gun style platformer that follows the eponymous title character as he battles bosses and collects the souls of runaway debtors after he loses a game of dice against the Devil. With the guidance of his grandfather Elder Kettle and the help of his brother Mugman, Cuphead will battle his way to salvation with slapstick glee. A visually sumptuous game, *Cuphead* evokes the golden age of American animation, with each hand-drawn element giving the game its distinctive aesthetic reminiscent of Popeye, early Mickey Mouse, or Felix the Cat. The soundtrack features a full jazz ensemble with bold brass and swinging rhythms. A celebration and love letter to the animation style and music of the Jazz Age, this challenging game is just as much fun to look at as it is to play.

Porcelain and Peppermint

This mocktail is inspired by the hero's recognizable cuphead that is filled with milk and garnished with a jaunty red-and-white straw. Cuphead's youthful recklessness makes this mint-forward drink feel both familiar and bold at the same time. Besides, after a couple of boss battles, it's nice to just relax with a freshly frothed cup of tea.

YIELD: 1 MOCKTAIL

3 ounces strongly brewed iced black tea

1 ounce heavy cream

½ ounce mint simple syrup (see page 18)

1 peppermint stick, for garnish

Combine the iced tea, cream, and mint syrup in a shaker, then top with ice. Shake until frosty, then strain the liquid back into the small tin. Shake for another 15 seconds, until frothy, and pour into an Irish coffee mug. Garnish with a red and white peppermint stick.

Bonus Round: Looking for a cozy variation? Use hot tea instead of iced and use either the steamer wand of an espresso machine or an electric milk frother to create a nice foam. Avoid shaking hot drinks in your cocktail shaker, as that's an easy way to end up with burned hands and a big mess.

Easter Egg

With more than thirty boss battles in the game, *Cuphead* holds the world record for most boss battles in any run-and-gun game.

Astral Cookies

In Cuphead's 2022 DLC "The Delicious Last Course," the plot of the expansion kicks off with the introduction of a special magical cookie that allows a disembodied spirit, Ms. Chalice, to switch places with Cuphead or his brother Mugman, with her restored to corporeality. When you're on a quest to reunite Ms. Chalice with her body and save both brothers, these cookies are a sweet treat. Whip up a batch the next time you're playing co-op or for any game-themed party—they're good enough to take you to another plane of existence!

YIELD: 48 COOKIES

1 cup (2 sticks) unsalted butter, softened

1 cup light brown sugar

½ cup granulated sugar

2 large eggs

2 teaspoons aromatic bitters

2¼ cups all-purpose flour

1 teaspoon baking soda

1 teaspoon salt

1½ cups butterscotch chips

1½ cups semisweet chocolate chips

Preheat the oven to 350 degrees F.

With an electric mixer, cream the butter and sugars until light and fluffy. Add the eggs and bitters and stir to combine. Fold in the flour, baking soda, and salt until just combined. Stir in the butterscotch and chocolate chips. Shape the dough into walnut-size balls and place on a rimmed baking sheet, 12 to a sheet. Bake for 10 to 12 minutes, until golden brown.

Hot tip: Angostura bitters are available in 4-ounce and 16-ounce bottles. If you're just using a few dashes at a time for a cocktail or mocktail, the small option works well, but for drinks like the V-Buck (page 156), or recipes like Astral Cookies, a larger bottle is the right call. You can remove the dasher top to pour and then pop it back on for the next time you need to measure in dashes.

Hades

There is no escape. A modern classic and beloved roguelike adventure, 2020's *Hades* follows Zagreus, Prince of the Underworld, as he fights his way to the surface in a desperate attempt to escape the prison of his youth and find his place in the cosmic order and family of gods. Highly acclaimed among industry professionals and players alike, this roguelike is noted for its especially robust dialogue trees, making each escape attempt fresh and giving you lots of extra exploration after the main story has been completed. Be prepared to die, *a lot*, and to be oh so happy when you crawl out of the river Styx to Hypnos's cheerful greeting.

Pom of Power

"Oh! A Pom of Power!" As you traverse the wilds of the Underworld doing battle with monsters and shades, there will come a time when you need to become stronger, to align yourself with the will of the gods who've blessed you, and to kick some spectral ass. Unlike the pomegranate that bound Persephone to Hades, this Underworld fruit holds the seeds of escape. This otherworldly mocktail is sweetened with pomegranate grenadine and spiced with warming herbal tea. Stir one up at the start of your run and you'll be on the surface in no time!

YIELD: 1 MOCKTAIL

3 ounces iced spice tea

¾ ounce Grenadine (page 19)

2 to 4 dashes grapefruit bitters

1 grapefruit peel, for garnish

Combine the iced tea, grenadine, and bitters in a mixing glass, then top with ice. Stir for 20 seconds, then strain into an old-fashioned glass over a single large ice cube. Garnish with an expressed grapefruit peel (see box on page 43).

Barge of Death

In the fiery waters of the River Phlegethon, there is a boat . . . and it wants to kill you. Better battle your way to safety on the farther shore. A fan-favorite mini-boss (including for this author), the Barge of Death really lets you indulge in some major crashing and bashing, while avoiding the constant fire damage that gives the Asphodel chambers their challenging flare. This drink is a spicy anise-laced riff on a daiquiri, perfect for the endearingly earnest and fun-loving prince of the underworld, Zagreus.

YIELD: 1 COCKTAIL

2 ounces white rum

1 ounce fresh lime juice, lime half reserved for garnish

½ ounce ouzo

½ ounce Grenadine (page 19)

1 bar spoon Hot Chili Tincture (page 22)

Sparkling wine

½ ounce overproof rum, for garnish

Combine the white rum, lime juice, ouzo, grenadine, and chili tincture in a shaker, then add ice. Shake for 15 seconds, until frosty, then strain into a large stemmed cocktail glass. Top with sparkling wine and garnish with your very own Barge of Death (see box).

Garnish Game: Barge of Death

Cut a lime in half crosswise, then juice to use in your cocktail. Be gentle, as you want to save half of the lime for the garnish. Fill the hollow lime half with ½ ounce overproof rum, hot as Asphodel! Float the rum-filled lime half in your cocktail, then use a lighter to ignite it—and that's the Barge of Death!

Cult of the Lamb

Come for the crashing and bashing through the forest as you crush the heretics of your fallen church; stay because your loyal followers need you desperately. This indie roguelike combines the cozy and the macabre as you play as a lamb saved from the sacrificial altar and tasked with forming a new cult in honor of the One Who Waits. Fans of cosmic horror with a whimsical twist will appreciate the charm of this game: the devoted cult followers have cute animal forms and the monsters of the Old Faith are appropriately gruesome. *Cult of the Lamb* debuted in 2022 to popular acclaim and has been celebrated for its replay value, a critical component of a top-quality roguelike.

Grassy Gruel

The description of this food item in the game is . . . unappetizing to put it mildly, but our cult followers deserve only the best. With that in mind, this cocktail is a crushed ice summer sour with a vegetal aroma and frosty refreshing bite. Cachaça, a sugarcane distillate from Brazil, is marked by its intense grassy flavor, very fresh and green. Paired with monk-made green chartreuse and lamb-friendly oat syrup, this layered sour will have your devotion. We pray the lamb be merciful!

YIELD: 1 COCKTAIL

1¼ ounces unaged cachaça

¾ ounce oat syrup (see page 18)

½ ounce green chartreuse

1 ounce fresh lime juice

1 lime wheel, for garnish

Combine the cachaça, oat syrup, chartreuse, and lime juice in a shaker, along with crushed ice. Shake for 10 seconds, then pour into a double old-fashioned glass over fresh crushed ice. Garnish with the lime wheel.

Castlevania

Since 1986, the *Castlevania* franchise has blossomed from a straightforward platform game to more open-ended role-playing exploration, while retaining the focus on combat and monster-hunting. Count Dracula resurrects each 100 years, seeking dominion over the earth, but the Belmonts, a clan of vampire hunters, enter Castle Dracula generation upon generation to do battle with the forces of darkness. An essential franchise that alongside *Metroid* inspired a thriving subgenre, this series brings thrills, chills, and vampire kills.

Life Apple

Known as the Wonder Drug of Life in the Japanese version of *Castlevania: Symphony of the Night*, this miraculous fruit fully restores life after death. The magical medicine is specific to the 1997 game, a fan favorite that casts Dracula's half-vampire son Alucard in the lead role as he investigates the titular castle after a five-year slumber. The drink won't fully restore your health, but it is a complex stirred concoction with fruity undertones, and that's the next best thing. As you confront the creatures of the night, there is no better companion.

YIELD: 1 COCKTAIL

1½ ounces apple brandy

½ ounce blood orange liqueur

½ ounce maraschino liqueur

½ ounce Peach Shrub (page 20)

2 to 4 dashes cardamom bitters

1 cocktail cherry (see box), for garnish

Combine the brandy, liqueurs, shrub, and bitters in a mixing glass and top with ice. Stir for 20 seconds, then strain into a stemmed cocktail glass. Garnish with the cocktail cherry.

Garnish Game: Cocktail Cherries

The cocktail cherry is the quintessential garnish. Neon-red ice cream cherries often taste more like the color red than genuine cherry—a tasty treat, but an experience that can be elevated with a different variety of garnish cherry. Instead, look for a high-quality cherry, like Luxardo or Fabbri Amarena, or for a lightly boozy twist, Woodford Reserve Bourbon Cherries. These cherries are soaked in either their own syrup or bourbon for a rich, fruity garnish that will add depth of flavor to every drink you mix. They last on the bar cart for months and can be refrigerated to extend the life span even further. Plus, a splash of the syrup in your cocktail or a seltzer highball can add an extra cherry kick to your favorite drinks.

VISUAL NOVELS AND INTERACTIVE FICTION

Do you like pressing the A button? Then you'll love the visual novel genre of video games. These games trade daring battles and cutting-edge graphics for devilish mysteries and fiendish puzzles. A genre for storytellers, these games range from the family-friendly to the mature and have great replayability for fresh nuance and emotional resonance. Plus, there's always lots of wacky one-off characters to populate episodic story worlds.

Ace Attorney

"Objection!" The Ace Attorney series of video games started in 2001 with *Phoenix Wright: Ace Attorney*. Gameplay comprises two portions—an investigation and a trial (like gin and vermouth)—with the player taking the part of the defending attorney. Clever mysteries play out over three-day trials with plenty of evidence to weigh against the contradictions in witness testimony. When you finally see that villain break down, you know your client is safe. With a wacky cast of characters and cleverly constructed mysteries, Ace Attorney is an early 2000s series with a heart of gold.

The Miles Edgeworth MarTEAni

The demon prosecutor of the courtroom and Phoenix Wright's fiercest rival, Miles Edgeworth is a prosecutor of class and distinction. He'll have a cup of tea when he's working, but after a long day sparring with Wright, aka the Turnabout Terror, it's time for something a bit stronger. This is a nod to Edgeworth's favorite take on the classic martini.

YIELD: 1 COCKTAIL

1½ ounces London dry gin

1½ ounces dry vermouth

1 bar spoon tea syrup (see page 18)

1 lemon twist (see box on page 79), for garnish

Combine the gin, vermouth, and tea syrup in a mixing glass, then add ice. Stir for 20 seconds, then strain into a stemmed cocktail glass. Garnish with a thin twist of lemon peel.

BAR BYTES: SYRUPS

Why add a syrup to your martini? A syrup adds more than sweetness and flavor to drinks; it also adds texture. A small bar spoon of tea syrup will give your martini a richer body and sturdier mouthfeel. It adds the weight of . . . unnecessary feelings.

Easter Egg

Did you know that only the English and French translations of *Phoenix Wright: Ace Attorney* are fully localized? Most international versions of the game are set in Los Angeles, following the American localization, but the French version is set in Paris. An early case relying on time zones sets these two versions apart from the Japanese original!

The Fragrance of Dark Coffee

Godot, the mysterious rival prosecutor from the third Ace Attorney game *Trials and Tribulations*, loves nothing more than a cup of hot coffee. He claims to drink seventeen cups a day, but when it's time for a trial, it seems at least half of those get thrown across the courtroom at the beleaguered Phoenix Wright. Godot likes his brew hot and bitter, but we'll have a bit of sweetness in this hot toddy–style coffee cocktail.

YIELD: 1 COCKTAIL

2 ounces espresso or strongly brewed black coffee

1 ounce tequila

½ ounce cinnamon syrup (see page 18)

½ ounce Orgeat (page 23)

2 to 4 dashes aromatic bitters

1 cinnamon stick, for garnish

Combine the espresso, tequila, cinnamon syrup, orgeat, and bitters in a heatproof mug and stir to combine. Garnish with the cinnamon stick.

BAR BYTES: HOT DRINKS

A hot drink should be served hot, so make sure your drink stays the perfect temperature by preheating your glass. While you're making your cocktail, fill your cocktail glass with hot water. When it's time to serve, discard the water and enjoy your perfectly heated cocktail. Remember that hot drinks should have less alcohol than cold drinks, as the heat brings forward ethanol flavors.

Zero Escape

Zero Escape is the thinking person's visual novel series. This trilogy of visual novel puzzle games combines escape rooms with lengthy narrative portions as nine characters pit their will against a controlling mastermind. Each game brings a fresh twist to the formula, building an elaborate and cohesive cosmology. Series players will enjoy picking apart what is true science and what is pseudoscience as their decisions bring them to multiple game endings and deeper understanding of why they were brought together—and forced to escape.

Ice-9

A fictional substance in the world of Zero Escape, Ice-9 is a polymorph of water that remains frozen at 96 degrees F. Appearing in the series' first game, *Nine Hours, Nine Persons, Nine Doors (999)*, and a necessary component for arriving at the game's True ending, this substance could bring about a total Ice Age and the end of the world. Fortunately, it's not something we need to worry about in our reality. The cocktail, on the other hand, is a frosty frozen concoction for the sophisticated set. We have plenty of thyme to escape Zero's machinations!

YIELD: 1 COCKTAIL

2 thyme sprigs, divided

1½ ounces absinthe

¾ ounce Orgeat (page 23)

1 ounce seltzer

Muddle 1 thyme sprig in the bottom of an old-fashioned glass, then top with crushed ice. Add the absinthe and orgeat and stir to combine. Top with the seltzer and garnish with the remaining thyme sprig.

BAR BYTES: MUDDLING

Be gentle with your herbs: that is the first law of muddling. Muddling is a technique used to express fresh flavors from berries, herbs, and fruit. A gentle touch is required: if you're too aggressive, it's easy to bruise whatever it is you're muddling and release bitter compounds. When buying a muddler, look for something that has a flat bottom instead of teeth and gently press the material, rotating the muddler around the base of the shaker or mixing glass. You will need to double-strain a cocktail or mocktail with muddled ingredients if you don't want flecks of muddled mint in your cocktail glass.

Danganronpa

This series of visual novels pairs Daily Life, Deadly Life, and Class Trial sections in an exciting adventure game. You play as a student at an elite high school along with a group of "Ultimate" classmates, each of whom is at the absolute pinnacle of their skill. There's no Ultimate Bartender, but then again, they are only high school students. You *can* meet the Ultimate Gambler and the Ultimate Astronaut, though, so maybe there's hope for us after all! But all is not well at Hope's Peak Academy, and the sinister teddy bear Monokuma has instigated the killing game: trapping all the students in the school and forcing them to commit and solve murders for any possibility of escape. The ultimate battle between hope and despair hinges on your investigations. A real highlight of the series is the juxtaposition of daily life with the murder mysteries, allowing you to form deeper relationships with the large cast of characters, explore the environment, and expand the story between murders. It makes it all the harder and more satisfying when you see a beloved character coerced into participating in the killing game!

KoMaiTaiDa

Nagito Komaeda is perhaps the most iconic character of the Danganronpa franchise. As the Ultimate Lucky Student, he appears in the second game of the series, *Danganronpa 2: Goodbye Despair*, and serves as the game's antagonist (a role far different from the mastermind). Komaeda drives the action of the game, making trouble for his fellow students as he explores the interplay of darkest despair and brightest hope. A game with a tropical setting needs a tropical drink, and our riff on a mai tai is no exception. Danganronpa is known for its distinctive splatters of pink blood, but I'd rather have guava nectar! I *hope* you like the KoMaiTaiDa; if not, I'll be lost to *despair*.

YIELD: 1 COCKTAIL

2 ounces rum

¾ ounce fresh lime juice

½ ounce guava nectar

½ ounce Orgeat (page 23)

1 lime wheel, for garnish

1 mint sprig, for garnish

Combine the rum, lime juice, guava nectar, and orgeat in a mixing glass, then add a small scoop of crushed ice. Shake for 10 seconds, then pour into a double old-fashioned glass filled with fresh crushed ice. Garnish with the lime wheel and mint sprig.

Hard Mode: Build your cocktail with 1 ounce white rum, then float 1 ounce blackstrap rum on top (see box on page 126) for the ultimate battle between hope and despair.

Disco Elysium

God does roll dice with the universe in this 2019 game. Make use of the anthropomorphized skills and personal convictions rattling around in your head as an amnesiac detective tasked with solving a murder mystery. Skill checks carry the player through the dialogue-heavy game, set in the muddy and slush-capped city of Revachol. Development of different skills, thoughts, and political alignments allow for replayability and fresh discoveries with each new game. The game has garnered universal acclaim for its story, gameplay, and distinctive oil paint aesthetic.

A Morning in Martinaise

A chilling environment of slush, mud, and deprivation greets you in *Disco Elysium*. Confusion reigns and with it the need for a stabilizing cocktail. Genever, a malt-based cousin of gin, takes the place of the game's Pale aged vodka, and red wine stains your lips as red as your nose. Bitter angst and yet . . . the hope of your partner, the sweetness of his company. Like the game that inspired it, this drink will not appeal to everyone, but for those who love it, oh do they love it.

YIELD: 1 COCKTAIL

1 teaspoon sugar, for rim

1½ ounces genever

1 ounce red wine syrup (see page 18)

1 ounce strongly brewed coffee

4 dashes orange bitters

Rim the edge of your glass with sugar (see page 40)—it's better than amphetamine! Splash the genever, wine syrup, coffee, and bitters in a rocks glass over a large ice cube and stir to combine. Knock it back and return to your partner, Detective.

Kentucky Route Zero

An indie point-and-click adventure game, 2020's *Kentucky Route Zero* follows a truck driver named Conway as he travels down the titular road, a mysterious and surreal state highway in the Bluegrass State. Like *Colossal Cave Adventure*, this game is set in south-central Kentucky, in the vicinity of Mammoth Cave, and demonstrates the possibilities of interactive fiction and the narrative power of video game storytelling. The journey is a movement through time and through space, a plot in and of itself, as the character encounters and interacts with the world around him. You cannot help being changed by the world of the open road.

Bourbon Slush

Everybody knows the mint julep, but my favorite Kentucky cocktail is probably the bourbon slush. On a hot summer evening, looking out over a field flickering with fireflies, there's nothing like a frosty, freezy bourbon slush. In *Kentucky Route Zero*, strange farms and mysterious forests proliferate the road, marvelously atmospheric and limned with tragedy. A comforting drink that will delight at home or in parts unknown, the bourbon slush is as true to the Bluegrass State as a drink can be.

YIELD: 1 COCKTAIL

1½ ounces bourbon whiskey

1 ounce fresh orange juice

1 ounce iced tea

¾ ounce fresh lemon juice

½ ounce mint simple syrup (see page 18)

1 mint sprig, for garnish

Combine the bourbon, orange juice, iced tea, lemon juice, and mint syrup in a blender, then add ice. Blend until frosty, then pour into a tall glass. Garnish with the mint sprig.

BAR BYTES: PLAYING WITH THE FORMAT

The bourbon slush is versatile and open-ended, so try adding some pineapple juice or a splash of amaretto. You can also play with the ratios—making your slush stronger, sweeter, sharper, whatever suits the mood. In the numinous and mysterious world of the hidden road, you can find a bourbon slush that suits every need. It also scales up well. *Kentucky Route Zero* is a single-player game, but you can whip up a batch for the whole party.

PUZZLE GAMES

Logic, pattern recognition, tile manipulation, and cognition, puzzle games are filled with brain teasers and problems to solve. Quick thinking will serve you well in this genre of games that ranges from fiendishly simple and elegant to wildly complex real-world physics. Keep your wits about you and you're sure to win the day. Or at least the high score . . .

Tetris

In the mid-'80s, something wonderful was brewing behind the Iron Curtain: a puzzle game that would capture the minds and dreams of millions. A game that is elegant in its simplicity but fiendish in its complexity, *Tetris* is a classic's classic. We've all played *Tetris* or one of the game's many clones and many are familiar with the "Tetris effect," where after a long session with the game you continue to see the Tetriminoes floating behind your eyes, playing the game on the most intimate console of all.

Tetrimino Jell-O Shots

The Tetriminoes are all composed of four-square tiles, creating seven orientations to slot together. Their elegance is in their simplicity, and the frustration of being stuck with a hollow in the middle of the board is maddening. Get your Tetriminoes in a row with this delicious party treat. I recommend making at least two batches with different flavors and colors. Variety is the spice of life!

YIELD: 8 JELL-O SHOTS

1½ cups vodka

½ cup boiling water

⅓ cup flavored liqueur, such as Raspberry Liqueur (page 22), blue curaçao, crème de violette, or Midori

3 (¾-ounce) envelopes unflavored gelatin

Line a 9-inch square baking pan with plastic wrap, then spray the wrap with nonstick cooking spray. Combine the vodka, boiling water, liqueur, and gelatin in a 4-cup measuring cup and stir until the gelatin is fully dissolved. Pour the mixture into the prepared baking pan and refrigerate to set, 6 hours. Use the plastic wrap to lift the square of gelatin out of the pan and place on a cutting board. Use a paring knife to cut out your Tetriminoes. Remember that gelatin is a difficult medium, so be kind to yourself.

Easy Mode: Skip the unflavored gelatin and liqueurs and make your Jell-O shots with flavors of Jell-O available at the grocery store. There are lots of options for the classic colors: Berry Blue, Lemon, Lime, Cherry, Grape, or Orange. The colors of the Tetriminoes were not standardized until the early 2000s, so have some fun with your flavors. Just don't make your Tetrimino Jell-O Shots grayscale! No one wants that at a cocktail party.

Myst

This classic adventure puzzle game debuted for PC in 1993 and focused on nonlinear storytelling and logical puzzles that encourage patience, introspection, and clever thinking. The player is pulled into the world of Myst Island by reading a book and there finds a series of puzzles and yet more books, which were traps for Sirrus and Achenar, the heirs to the island. The player must uncover the mysterious history of the family and their legacy. The legacy of the game is similarly storied, with *Myst* garnering widespread praise when it debuted, and noted for the environmental storytelling, complicated morality, and pairing of form and function. A game for casual players without the constraints of time, *Myst* was a major influence on both later puzzle games and exploration games.

Sirrus and Achenar

A red book, a blue book, a secret green book . . . the mysteries of Myst Island are many, and somewhere between different points of view lies the truth. The original game sees the player charged with piecing together which of two brothers, each trapped in a book, is guilty of the destruction of Myst Island's library and which is innocent. The two brothers complement each other, as do the red and blue sweeteners in this effervescent elevated sour.

YIELD: 2 COCKTAILS

6 fresh mint leaves

3 ounces white rum

2 ounces fresh lime juice

½ ounce Raspberry Liqueur (page 22)

½ ounce blue curaçao

Sparkling wine

Gently muddle 4 mint leaves in the bottom of a shaker. Add the rum, lime juice, raspberry liqueur, and curaçao, then ice. Strain into 2 large coupes and top with sparkling wine. Garnish each with a single mint leaf.

Expert Mode: Try splitting the drink, shaking up half the lime and rum with raspberry liqueur and half with blue curaçao. See how each half tastes separately and how they compare with the combined whole.

Professor Layton

Puzzles and mysteries are always at this archeologist and gentleman scholar's fingertips, and the distinguished Professor Hershel Layton solves puzzles with aplomb. Aided by his bright and clever apprentice, Luke Triton, Professor Layton solves brain teasers from logic puzzles and mazes to tessellations and memory matching. There are six main sequence games, an original trilogy, and a prequel trilogy, plus several spinoffs and a new main sequence game in the works: *Professor Layton and the New World of Steam*. This is a perfect series for gamers of all ages who want to challenge their puzzle-solving skills amid an eccentric cast and picturesque setting.

Hershel Layton's Top Hat

Professor Layton is seldom seen without his signature top hat. It is his emblem, the sign on his door, the seal on his correspondence, the symbol of all the good professor stands for. As he says in *Professor Layton and the Unwound Future*, "Is there any greater proof of one's gentlemanly nature than a fine top hat?" This mocktail is almost as tall as the professor's hat, with a distinguished froth for an afternoon of puzzle solving.

YIELD: 1 MOCKTAIL

4 ounces strongly brewed iced black tea

½ ounce Simple Syrup (page 17) made with demerara sugar

¼ ounce vanilla extract

2 to 4 dashes orange bitters

1 bar spoon whole milk powder

Seltzer

Combine the iced tea, simple syrup, vanilla, bitters, and milk powder in a shaker. Stir to combine, then dry shake for 15 seconds. Add ice and shake for another 15 seconds. Double-strain into a highball glass and top with seltzer.

BAR BYTES: ALTERNATIVE FOAMING AGENTS

When making fizzes, you may often use egg white instead of whole milk powder. This is a good choice for cocktails, where citrus and alcohol will "cook" the egg white, but for mocktails, it is safer and wiser to stick with whole milk powder.

Easter Egg

Not only does Professor Layton owe a portion of his origins to the popularity of *Phoenix Wright: Ace Attorney*, but the two franchises have a shared crossover game. *Professor Layton vs. Phoenix Wright: Ace Attorney* makes allies and occasional rivals of the debonair professor and determined defense attorney as they find themselves in a mysterious village gripped by a terror of witches.

Portal

A spinoff of the first-person shooter Half-Life games, this puzzle-platform game debuted in 2007 and was followed by a sequel in 2011. The Portal series follows Chell, the unfortunate main character who is made to solve puzzles and move through rooms by the wickedly taunting artificial intelligence GLaDOS. With portal gun in hand, Chell can create wormholes throughout her environment, allowing the player to move through the environment in innovative physics-based play. A classic series of the 2000s, the Portal games are landmark titles in the world of puzzle-solving games.

The Cake Is a Lie

This is not a cake. This is a cocktail. You cannot have any cake. The cake is a lie. A recurring element in Portal, the cake is an unattainable goal. Modeled on a black forest cake, GLaDOS uses the cake to taunt and tempt the character. Our drink is a marriage of chocolate and cherry and while it may not be a cake, I hope it is a better prize than you would find at Aperture Labs.

YIELD: 1 COCKTAIL

1 ounce cognac

1 ounce dark crème de cacao

1 ounce heavy cream

½ ounce maraschino liqueur

½ ounce cherry grenadine (see page 19)

1 cocktail cherry (see box on page 53), for garnish

Combine the cognac, crème de cacao, cream, maraschino liqueur, and grenadine in a shaker, then add ice. Shake for 15 seconds, then strain the liquid back into the small tin. Discard the ice and shake for a further 15 seconds (reverse dry shake—see box on page 73). Pour into a stemmed cocktail glass and garnish with the cocktail cherry.

Candy Crush Saga

An iconic puzzle game and beloved mobile classic, *Candy Crush Saga* debuted for iOS and Android in 2012. Swapping candy-shaped tiles to match sets of three items, *Candy Crush Saga* is marked both by colorful characters and its addictive gameplay, with levels that are quick and satisfying but always leave you wanting more. With more than 14,000 levels, you can keep swapping those candies to your heart's content.

A Sweet Reward!

Chocolate is more often an obstacle than a reward in *Candy Crush Saga*, but this dessert cocktail is definitely more treat than trouble. Reminiscent of an Almond Joy, this is the perfect drink to sip on as you enjoy a level or twenty of your favorite match-three adventure.

YIELD: 1 COCKTAIL

1 ounce blackstrap rum

1 ounce heavy cream

½ ounce dark crème de cacao

½ ounce Orgeat (page 23)

½ ounce cream of coconut

Combine all the ingredients in a shaker, then add ice. Shake for 15 seconds, then strain the liquid back into the small tin. Discard the ice and shake for another 15 seconds (reverse dry shake—see box). Pour into a stemmed cocktail glass and enjoy.

BAR BYTES: THE REVERSE DRY SHAKE

The reverse dry shake and its companion technique, the dry shake (see box on page 35), are useful in adding airy volume to fizzes and dessert cocktails. The reverse dry shake doesn't give quite as much volume as the dry shake, but it is a lot easier to learn and often less messy. To reverse dry shake, combine all your ingredients in a shaker and add ice. Shake until chilled (this is the wet shake). Strain the liquid back into the small tin and discard the ice. Then cap your shaker again and shake until frothed and foamed. Strain into a cocktail glass and enjoy.

The reason the reverse dry shake is preferable to the dry shake is a matter of temperature. The wet shake with ice chills the shaker tins, and when the metal cools, it contracts. You'll have an easier time sealing and unsealing your tins for the more aggressive dry shake when they are already chilled! With puzzle games, the right sequence of events is critical to your solving success.

SIMULATION GAMES

Simulation games are a big tent. Whether you want to live a cozy life on a deserted island, raise cities and families, farm, fish, or just explore, there's a simulation title for you. With a range of experiences from comforting to harrowing, a simulation game lets you put your feet in someone else's shoes for a while, to strategize or just to vibe.

The Sims

A series of life simulation games, *The Sims* allows you to rule as a god over your subjects: placing them in houses and tending to their needs, their relationships, their decorations, and their devotions. Each game expands the emotions of your Sims, the actions they can take, and the lives you can build for them. A game that can be perfectly casual or entrancingly obsessive, there have been dozens of expansions and compilation packs for each game in the series, making this one of the most expansive franchises in the history of video gaming. What will you do with your Sims?

Mouthwatering Beauty Cocktail

A crisp mocktail made with the Main Squeezer 235X, this drink will fill your Sims' hunger bar and quench your thirst. In the game, this drink is a love potion, so make two and share with someone you care about.

YIELD: 1 MOCKTAIL

3 cucumber slices, divided

2 ounces fresh orange juice

1 ounce fresh lime juice

½ ounce Grenadine (page 19)

4 ounces seltzer

Gently muddle 2 cucumber slices in the bottom of a shaker. Add the orange juice, lime juice, and grenadine, then top with ice. Shake for 10 seconds, until frosty, then strain into a highball glass over fresh ice. Top with the seltzer and garnish with the remaining cucumber slice.

+1 Alcohol: Add 1 ounce gin to your shaker along with the fruit juice and grenadine.

Animal Crossing: New Horizons

How many of us dream of moving to a small town where life is simpler; where there are fossils to find, insects and fish to catch, and cheerful neighbors to help and visit? The dream is made reality in *Animal Crossing*, first released in 2001 and then followed by its four sequels, including most recently many a gamer's pandemic comfort game: *Animal Crossing: New Horizons*, which debuted in the advent of the COVID-19 pandemic. This popular simulation game is open-ended and easy-going, encouraging customization and exploration. The games are played in real time, with events and seasons matching the world beyond the game. When you're stuck inside, it's nice to imagine a kinder, safer world outdoors, which is why this game is an enduring favorite for the whole family.

Garden Party

A new life awaits on a desert island, and a certain crafty tanuki has everything you need to set up in style. Your travel agent and the director of resident services, this fellow knows just what you need and how much it costs. Make this drink with Old Tom gin, a sweeter, more approachable style of gin, and you'll be honoring the tanuki who makes all things possible: Mr. Tom Nook.

YIELD: 1 COCKTAIL

1 ounce gin

¾ ounce fresh lemon juice

½ ounce St-Germain elderflower liqueur

½ ounce Raspberry Liqueur (page 22)

½ ounce dry vermouth

Sparkling wine

3 raspberries, for garnish

1 lemon twist (see box), for garnish

Combine the gin, lemon juice, liqueurs, and vermouth in a shaker, then top with ice. Shake until frosty, then strain into a stemmed cocktail glass. Top with sparkling wine and garnish with the raspberries and lemon twist.

Garnish Game: The Perfect Twist

Using a vegetable peeler, paring knife, or twist peeler, cut into the citrus fruit and rotate the fruit away from you. If you use a vegetable peeler, you will end up with a broader swath and might choose to cut your peel into several thinner twists. When you are satisfied with the size of your peel, curl the twist tightly around a chopstick and set aside while you make the cocktail or mocktail. Then, pull the peel off the chopstick and enjoy the springiest twist of them all!

Dear Esther

An exploration game set in the Hebridean Islands of Scotland, *Dear Esther* is a marvel of immersion and storytelling. It's almost a visual novel and an important entry in the walking simulator genre, but with more flexibility as you explore your surroundings. Gameplay is minimalistic, but thematic depth and emotional resonance dominate. A portrait of grief, this game is a true work of art and demonstrates the unity of form and function to tell a story of moving intimacy that leaves the player connected both to the island and to the anonymous narrator. For gamers who love the storytelling possibilities of a game, *Dear Esther* is not to be missed.

Atholl Brose

A traditional Scottish drink, this cocktail is a cup of comfort on a cold night. *Dear Esther* is mournful and melancholy, isolated amid the lonely watches of the Hebrides. And with the implication that Esther, the title character, perished in a mysterious incident, it seems only right to offer a mocktail version of the classic mixed drink.

YIELD: 1 MOCKTAIL

2 ounces Oatmeal Brose (page 19)

1 ounce heavy cream

¾ ounce honey syrup (see page 18)

2 to 4 dashes aromatic bitters

Combine all the ingredients in a shaker, then top with ice. Shake for 15 seconds, then strain the liquid back into the small tin. Discard the ice and shake for another 15 seconds (reverse dry shake—see box on page 73). Pour into a stemmed cocktail glass and enjoy.

+1 Alcohol: Add 1 ounce blended Scotch whisky. It's easy to spend a lot of money on Scotch, but cocktails work best with middle-of-the-road spirits, because the cocktail should be greater than the sum of its parts. You don't need to use an ounce of your finest single-malt Islay or Speyside Scotch, especially because truly great Scotch whisky will overpower all the other ingredients in your drink.

Firewatch

An adventure simulation game released in 2016, *Firewatch* follows a fire lookout in Shoshone National Forest in the late '80s. In this quiet game, Henry is largely alone and can communicate with his supervisor, Delilah, only via walkie-talkie, a choice that is optional to the player. A sense of mystery and an atmosphere of paranoia pervade the game, as Henry investigates his predecessor and the secrets of the forest that surrounds his lookout tower. Tense and immersive, *Firewatch* is a must-play for nature lovers and visual novel fans who want a more involved style of gameplay. Completion of the story allows the player to explore the map in an open world format, suitable to those who just like to wander among the trees.

Wildfire Wood

It's lonely out in the woods, and a slow-sipping cocktail is a great way to wind down after a day of watching for wildfires and exploration of the surrounding forest. Smoke, spice, and a touch of heat meet in this rich cocktail ideal for an evening by the campfire or as a guard against the chill of the night. It's a woodsy warmth that you can savor, sipping as you explore the wilds around you.

YIELD: 1 COCKTAIL

2 ounces rye whiskey

½ ounce lapsang souchong syrup
(see "tea syrup" on page 18)

½ ounce maple syrup

2 to 4 dashes black walnut or toasted pecan bitters

1 bar spoon Hot Chili Tincture (page 22)

1 praline pecan (see box on page 82),
for garnish

Combine the rye, tea syrup, maple syrup, bitters, and chili tincture in a rocks glass over a large ice cube. Stir to combine, then garnish with the praline pecan.

Garnish Game: Praline Pecans

1 egg white	2 cups pecans
1 tablespoon cold water	¾ cup demerara sugar
1 tablespoon angostura bitters	½ teaspoon kosher salt

Preheat the oven to 275 degrees F. Line a rimmed baking sheet with parchment paper.

In a small bowl, whisk together the egg white, cold water, and bitters until frothy. Toss the pecans in the egg mixture, then stir in the sugar and salt.

Spread out the pecans in a single layer on the prepared baking sheet. Bake for 1 hour, flipping the pecans halfway through. Allow to cool, then enjoy as a snack and a garnish. Store in an airtight container at room temperature for up to 1 month.

BAR BYTES: SWIZZLING

The swizzle is the stir that approximates a shake. Traditionally the swizzle is performed with a swizzle stick, a branch of the Caribbean swizzle tree that flares at the base into a starlike pattern. If you don't want to purchase a swizzle stick and don't have a swizzle tree in your backyard, you can use your bar spoon instead or, in a pinch, even a chopstick, but that will take a lot more work. To swizzle a drink, put your swizzle stick (or bar spoon) in your cocktail. Rub the swizzle stick between your palms, rotating it through the glass and raising it up and down along the length of the glass. You want your ingredients to mix and blend. When you're satisfied with the mixing of your swizzle, remove the swizzle stick and start sipping!

Stardew Valley

A true indie darling, *Stardew Valley* is a modern classic and the game to set the cozy gaming trend. The farming RPG debuted in 2016 and has now sold more than 20 million copies. At the start of the game, your grandfather leaves you a small farm in his will, allowing an escape from the hustle and bustle of the city for a quiet life in the country. Or not so quiet, as there's always work to do on the farm, the town is facing a turning point, and oh yeah, your grandfather's ghost will be back after a few years to evaluate how you've managed the farm in his absence. Better get to work! Farming is the core of the game, but you'll stay for the chance to befriend and romance the villagers of the valley, and as the seasons pass, you'll fall more and more in love with the rhythm of life in the whimsical valley.

Stardrop Swizzle

A magical berry found in Stardew Valley, the Stardrop tastes like your favorite food and grants you greater strength and endurance, making it easier to spend your day farming, foraging, mining, and fishing. Stardrops may not be real, but star fruit (aka carambola) is, and the tropical fruit takes center stage in this refreshing cocktail perfect for summer nights under the stars after a long day.

YIELD: 1 COCKTAIL

1 star fruit, thinly sliced

2 ounces pineapple juice

1½ ounces aged rum

1 ounce fresh lime juice

½ ounce Orgeat (page 23)

¼ ounce blue curaçao

¼ ounce Ginger Syrup (page 21)

Gently muddle 2 star fruit slices in the bottom of a swizzle or hurricane glass. Top with crushed ice, then the pineapple juice, rum, lime juice, orgeat, curaçao, and ginger syrup. Swizzle (see box on page 83) until blended and frost forms on the exterior of the glass, then top with fresh crushed ice and garnish with another slice of star fruit.

Stardew Valley Cheeseboard

Stardew Valley celebrates the bounty of agriculture and at a party, nothing says abundance and variety quite like a cheeseboard. A wide selection of little snacks and nibbly bits will give your guests something to feast on between rounds of gameplay and over many happy hours of conversation.

When I'm setting up a cheeseboard, I like to follow a little rule: something soft, something hard, something smoky, and something spicy. This helps me prepare a board that will satisfy all the cheese lovers at my party. After I have my cheeses in place, I think about what some nice accompaniments would be. Crackers are a must, but also an interesting honey, some jams, nuts, and pickled vegetables make a cheeseboard something special all year round. With the ever-changing selection of agricultural products throughout the year in Stardew Valley, no matter the weather you'll have the perfect selection of tasty treats for the whole party.

In Stardew Valley, our pigs dig truffles and our cows give milk, so this cheeseboard will be vegetarian friendly. For summer, I love to have some sun-dried tomatoes on my board, and honey is a must. In autumn, nice crisp apple slices and roasted nuts liven up my parties. See the following ideas of what to put on your seasonal cheeseboard. Remember, just as in the Grange Display at the Stardew Valley Fair, variety is your friend!

Spring Board: herbed Gouda, pepper jack, and goat cheeses, paired with dried apricots, cherries, pickled rhubarb, garlic butter, strawberries, or salted herring

Summer Board: herbed Gouda, pepper jack, and goat cheeses, paired with fresh peach slices, fresh grapes, dried blueberries, hot pepper relish, sun-dried tomatoes

Fall Board: smoked Gruyère, aged Gouda, and Brie cheeses, paired with apple slices, marinated artichoke hearts, pickled beets, dried cranberries, dried blackberries, dried plums, pumpkin butter, hazelnuts

Winter Board: smoked Gruyère, aged Gouda, and Brie cheeses, paired with jam, pickles, smoked trout, carrots, radishes (You can't grow crops in the winter unless you have a greenhouse, so now is the time to enjoy your pickled and preserved foods.)

ROLE-PLAYING GAMES

Follow your character on a journey, explore a world, and grow stronger as you face challenges and learn more. These are games with expansive settings, main quests and side quests, combat and crafting, and an array of items at your disposal. Whether you're playing in a fantasy kingdom, modern Tokyo, or the far reaches of space, an RPG offers an immersive experience for single-player and multiplayer gamers alike. And you'd better believe there's a fishing minigame!

The Legend of Zelda: Breath of the Wild

The nineteenth game in the Zelda franchise debuted in 2017 and tasks Link with the salvation of Hyrule in the wake of ten thousand years of degradation and a century of calamity. *Breath of the Wild* is unstructured, encouraging a nonlinear approach and exploration of the environment, including puzzle-filled shrines, an abundance of side quests, and plenty of items, armor, and weapons to collect. Physics puzzles and wide options for interacting with the world make each player's experience unique, and the interplay of natural scenery with ruins and devastation mark the game with thematic resonance and deep emotional appeal. The winner of more than two dozen major gaming awards, *Breath of the Wild* is a masterpiece entry in a landmark series.

Noble Pursuit

Every great bar needs a great signature cocktail! In Gerudo village, you'll find the Noble Canteen, and the drink there is the Noble Pursuit. The Perfect Drink quest requires Link to fetch the ice needed to make the beverage. As we've seen, ice is essential to all great cocktails and mocktails. Then, in spinoff game *Hyrule Warriors: Age of Calamity*, the Noble Pursuit can be made with 3 Palm Fruits, 3 Voltfruits, 3 Hydromelons, and 3 Rock Salts. Equal parts make for easy gaming but an overwhelming drink, so we've played with the ratios a bit, hopefully living up to the exacting standards of Furosa and the Noble Canteen.

YIELD: 1 COCKTAIL

2 ounces pineapple juice

1½ ounces aged rum

½ ounce Midori

½ ounce cream of coconut

½ ounce fresh lime juice

¼ ounce saline solution
(see box on page 91)

1 melon wedge, for garnish

Combine the pineapple juice, rum, Midori, cream of coconut, lime juice, and saline in a blender, then top with ice. Blend until frosty. Pour into a hurricane glass and garnish with a wedge of your favorite melon and a tropical umbrella.

Link's Pursuit

Furosa, the owner of the Noble Canteen, says that Link is too young to try her version of the Noble Pursuit, but the hero of Hyrule needs a refreshing beverage after running around and collecting ice. With that in mind, here's a mocktail version of the Noble Pursuit.

YIELD: 1 MOCKTAIL

3 ounces pineapple juice

1 ounce Melon Shrub (page 20)

¾ ounce cream of coconut

½ ounce fresh lime juice

¼ ounce saline solution (see box)

1 bar spoon Simple Syrup (page 17) made with demerara sugar

1 melon wedge, for garnish

Combine the pineapple juice, shrub, cream of coconut, lime juice, saline, and simple syrup in a blender, then top with ice. Blend until frosty. Pour into a hurricane glass and garnish with a wedge of your favorite melon and a tropical umbrella.

BAR BYTES: SALINE SOLUTION

To make a simple saline solution, mix ¼ cup kosher salt into 1 cup water until it dissolves. Store in an airtight container in the fridge for up to 3 months to add extra depth to your cocktails and mocktails.

Pokémon

Gotta catch 'em all! For nearly thirty years, gamers have been traversing the wilds of the Pokémon world, collecting strange creatures, battling rivals, and mastering the different types of creatures populating their neighborhood. With a starter Pokémon of Grass-type, Water-type, or Fire-type, your young trainer can set off on a journey to explore the world. Each game generation introduces a new region of the world, with new Pokémon endemic to their locality, along with a heavy dash of charm and whimsy. With nine generations of Pokémon, there is always a chance to make a new friend or collect your familiar favorite. And of course, Pikachu, the series mascot, is one of the most recognizable video game characters in the world!

Dratini

This mocktail was inspired by the colorful martinis of the 1990s and early 2000s that were more playful than the classic martini. A pale blush blue, like the adorable dragon-type Pokémon that lent the drink its name, the Dratini grows and sheds its skin, so feel free to top the drink with a splash of seltzer when you are running low and watch your Pokémon mocktail grow.

YIELD: 1 MOCKTAIL

¾ ounce blueberry grenadine (see page 19)

¾ ounce guava nectar

¾ ounce fresh lemon juice

¾ ounce lime cordial (see page 24)

1 bar spoon saline solution (see box on page 91)

1 lemon peel snake (see box on page 116), for garnish

Combine the grenadine, guava nectar, lemon juice, lime cordial, and saline in a shaker, then top with ice. Shake vigorously until chilled, then strain into a stemmed cocktail glass. Garnish with the lemon peel snake.

Skyrim

The fifth game in the Elder Scrolls series, this action RPG was released in 2011 to much love and support from fans. The fantasy land of the game is open to exploration with plenty of side quests and in-world jobs to accomplish. In this world of elves, orcs, and dragons, players must master combat and magical power alike, doing battle with various enemies, including the primary antagonist: the fearsome dragon Alduin. A single-player game, *Skyrim* offers plenty of NPCs and adventures to keep you on your toes.

Ashfire Mead

Ashfire mead is one of the iconic drinks from the world of Elder Scrolls and is perfect for regenerating your stamina. Mead is a fermented honey wine that has roots going back to almost neolithic times. Though it does not often appear in mixed drinks, honey syrup is an easy-to-source alternative for bringing that rich honey flavor to your cocktails and mocktails.

YIELD: 1 COCKTAIL

1 cedar strip

1½ ounces apple brandy

¾ ounce honey syrup (see page 18)

½ ounce sweet vermouth

¼ ounce lapsang souchong syrup (see "tea syrup" on page 18)

1 small piece honeycomb, for garnish

Smoke the interior of an old-fashioned glass with cedar (see box). Combine the brandy, honey syrup, vermouth, and tea syrup in a mixing glass, then top with ice. Stir for 20 seconds, until combined and chilled. Strain into the prepared glass over a large ice cube. Garnish with a small piece of honeycomb.

Garnish Game: Smoking a Glass

Light the edge of your cedar strip (available at many home brew stores). Shake gently so the flame is extinguished but the edge is still smoking. Place the smoking cedar strip on a heatproof plate, then place your glass upside down over the cedar strip. Airflow is the friend of smoke, so make sure that one edge of the glass is on the surface of the plate and one edge is on top of the cedar strip. Prepare the rest of your cocktail or mocktail. When it's time to serve, reinvert the cocktail glass, strain your drink into the glass, and fully extinguish the cedar strip with a gentle shake. This technique also works with cinnamon sticks.

Kingdom Hearts

A crossover adventure RPG of iconic Disney and Square Enix characters, this series pits its heroes against the forces of darkness. A mix of recognizable properties and unique worlds leads to a gaming experience unlike any other. Wield the Keyblade against the heartless and protect the interlinked worlds from the corrupting darkness. The hero Sora is joined by court wizard Donald Duck and knight captain Goofy in a mix of action, combat, and exploration.

Sea Salt Milkshake

Here's the ideal salty-sweet treat for sunset summers in Twilight Town. An emblem of friend-ship and a frosty dessert go hand in hand when you've battled your way through the world. Twilight Town, home to those souls and bodies that have lost their hearts, can be a melancholy place, but the sea salt ice cream can't be beat.

YIELD: 1 MOCKTAIL

2 ounces whole milk

1½ ounces heavy cream

1 ounce saline solution (see box on page 91)

¾ ounce Orgeat (page 23)

½ ounce Simple Syrup (page 17) made with demerara sugar

¼ ounce vanilla extract

Whipped cream, for garnish

1 cocktail cherry (see box on page 53), for garnish

Combine the milk, cream, saline, orgeat, simple syrup, and vanilla in a blender, then add ice. Blend until frosty, then pour into a tall glass. Garnish with a dollop of whipped cream and the cocktail cherry.

+1 Alcohol: Add 1½ ounces aged rum to make a delicious cocktail variation.

No Man's Sky

An open-world space opera with a procedurally generated universe you could spend a lifetime exploring, *No Man's Sky* debuted in 2016 and has captured imaginations ever since. This single-player game builds a community with each new documented planet—there are more than 18 quintillion to explore! While there's a story, the joy of *No Man's Sky* is the expansion and exploration. Nothing is more thrilling than seeing new flora and fauna, surviving vicious storms and poisonous atmospheres, and sitting outside your camp watching the distant stars shining down.

Exoplanet

No Man's Sky reimagines the spirit of adventure and exploration that captured the minds of writers, scientists, and citizens through the twentieth century. With new worlds to explore in the inky void of space, you may confront the chill between the stars and the wonder of an uncharted planet. Looking out to the stars in technicolor dreams of the 1960s and '70s inspired this bright cocktail.

YIELD: 1 COCKTAIL

1½ ounces gin

1 ounce fresh lemon juice

½ ounce Orgeat (page 23)

½ ounce passion fruit syrup

¼ ounce Ginger Syrup (page 21)

¼ ounce crème de violette

1 lemon peel, for garnish

1 cocktail cherry (see box on page 53), for garnish

Combine the gin, lemon juice, orgeat, passion fruit syrup, ginger syrup, and crème de violette in a swizzle or hurricane glass and add a scoop of crushed ice. Swizzle (see box on page 83). Top with another scoop of crushed ice and garnish with a ring planet (see box below).

Garnish Game: Ring Planet

Hold a lemon between your thumb and forefinger and, using a twist peeler or paring knife, cut, rotating the fruit away from you. Working your way around the lemon, cut one long piece of peel. Stick a cocktail pick through the peel halfway down, being careful not to break it. Next, skewer a cocktail cherry on the cocktail pick. Complete your garnish by pinning the two ends of the twist on the end of the cocktail pick to form a ring with the cherry resting in the middle. Place on the side of your drink and enjoy!

Easy Mode: Use a vegetable peeler to cut a wider swath of lemon peel, then wrap the lemon peel around the cocktail cherry and spear them together on a cocktail pick. Less a ring planet and more a ring moon, but just as delicious!

Mass Effect

This science fiction adventure trilogy places humans of the twenty-second century in a greater galactic context of aliens and artificial life-forms. The game's extensive dialogue trees offer paths in the main character's morality and the choice of being a Paragon or a Renegade. As players seek connection across the vast cosmos, the romance options are robust and have been celebrated for their recognition of same-sex as well as different-sex relationships. The power of science fiction to hope and to fight for justice burns bright in this essential RPG series.

Mass Relay

The pale blue light of the Mass Relay shines at the outer limits of the solar system, offering the promise of faster-than-light travel and a broader galaxy, with all its opportunities and dangers. It is the discovery of the Mass Relay that brings humanity into contact with the wider galactic community. Explore the Milky Way and the origins of our deepest connections between the stars.

YIELD: 1 COCKTAIL

1 ounce white rum

1 ounce heavy cream

¾ ounce blue curaçao

¼ ounce Ginger Syrup (page 21)

1 lemon peel, for garnish

1 cocktail cherry (see box on page 53), for garnish

Combine the rum, cream, curaçao, and ginger syrup in a shaker, then top with ice. Shake for 15 seconds, until chilled, then strain the liquid into the small tin of the shaker. Discard the ice and shake for another 15 seconds (reverse dry shake—see box on page 73). Strain into a stemmed cocktail glass and garnish with a ring planet (see box on page 98).

Undertale

Mercy is the name of the game in the 2015 indie RPG *Undertale*. A child wanders through the magical Underground, a realm inhabited by monsters and magical beings. The child's morality is the cornerstone of the game. The combat system is unique in that it allows the player to choose between battling through the entire game and defeating the creatures you encounter or instead subduing or pacifying them. The choices of violence or mercy change the game's progression, and there are three different endings available—including Pacifist, Alternate Neutral, and No Mercy for those gamers of a more . . . *combative* spirit and for the completionist as well. *Undertale* is a cult classic with unique encounters, memorable characters, and a compelling story that is not to be missed.

Blood and Sans

Early in the game you meet Sans, a skeleton guard with an easygoing, friendly vibe. But be careful, as he's stronger than he looks and his boss battle is one of the most challenging of the game. He's fond of puns, so a riff on the classic Blood and Sand Sour feels appropriate for him. Sans is from Snowdin, so this drink is perfectly suited to fresh crushed ice. Bittersweet and bright, this is a drink to celebrate the triumph of success or the perfection of peace.

YIELD: 1 COCKTAIL

1 ounce London dry gin

¾ ounce sweet vermouth

½ ounce maraschino liqueur

½ ounce fresh orange juice

¼ ounce lemon cordial (see page 24)

1 orange peel, for garnish

Combine the gin, vermouth, maraschino liqueur, orange juice, and lemon cordial in a shaker, then top with ice. Shake for 15 seconds, until frosty. Strain into an old-fashioned glass over fresh crushed ice. Garnish with the orange peel.

Easter Egg

Toby Fox, the creator of *Undertale*, also created a related game: *Deltarune*. The two games are not set in the same world but do share some characters and thematic elements, which seems fitting when you learn that the title is an anagram of *Undertale*.

Persona 5

A text-heavy RPG balanced with dungeon-crawling battles, this game follows the Joker, a Japanese teenager as he attends high school and fights as a member of the vigilante group Phantom Thieves of Hearts. Battles in the Metaverse rely on the use of personas, manifestations of the characters' inner spirit of rebellion, and the relationship between outward presentation and inner understanding. Figures from mythology, psychoanalytic principles, and the tarot have all played a role in the series, but in *Persona 5*, it is historical thieves and outlaws—masked men and women—who come to the fore. Character interactions feed strength in battle, and the fight for personal autonomy dominates the restrictions of age and social expectation.

Water of Rebirth

Whiskey is the aqua vitae, the water of life, a reviving drink. For the Phantom Thieves of *Persona 5*, a refreshing beverage from a vending machine is just the thing to restore health and spiritual wellness. Fortunately, unlike in the game, this drink *isn't* blended with placenta, but heavy cream adds depth and richness.

YIELD: 1 COCKTAIL

2 ounces strongly brewed coffee, chilled

1½ ounces Irish whiskey

1 ounce heavy cream

½ ounce cinnamon syrup (see page 18)

¼ ounce Ginger Syrup (page 21)

1 cinnamon stick, for garnish

Combine the coffee, whiskey, cream, and syrups in a blender, then add ice. Blend until frosty, then pour into a tall glass. Garnish with the cinnamon stick.

+1 Nonalcoholic: The Phantom Thieves are high school students, so in deference to them, you may wish to omit the whiskey.

Genshin Impact

A free-to-play, open-world action RPG with gacha mechanics, *Genshin Impact* debuted in 2020 and quickly gained a passionate fan base. Set in a fantasy world called Teyvat, which is governed by seven elemental nations, *Genshin Impact* is inspired by global cultures and Gnostic mysticism, with rich characterization and versatile combat. You play as a multiverse explorer known as the Traveler and wander across Teyvat battling monsters with a cast of over sixty unique and lovable characters.

Berry and Mint Burst

A robust food-crafting mechanism yields a delicious mocktail with freshly squeezed lemon. This drink will have you raring for a fight and boost your chance of dealing critical damage—just keep the battle in the game!

YIELD: 1 MOCKTAIL

6 blueberries, for drink and garnish

¾ ounce mint simple syrup (see page 18)

1 ounce fresh lemon juice

1 ounce strongly brewed iced green tea

Seltzer

1 mint sprig, for garnish

Muddle 3 blueberries and the mint syrup in the bottom of a shaker, then top with the lemon juice and green tea. Add ice and shake for 10 seconds. Strain into a hurricane glass over crushed ice and top with a splash of seltzer. Garnish with the remaining 3 blueberries and the mint sprig.

Elden Ring

This *Souls*-like RPG debuted in 2022. A dark fantasy world filled with danger and marked by a high difficulty player experience, *Elden Ring* is available primarily as a single-player game but also offers an online PvP and co-op mode for gamers looking for a multiplayer experience. Play as the Tarnished through an open world replete with hidden dungeons and magical items. The game is the union of Hidetaka Miyazaki and George R. R. Martin, pairing an austere narrative focused on gameplay with deep lore underpinning the story. Don't expect much of a helping hand, with either the lore or the gameplay, as there's no easy mode to be found! At the end of a session, you might find yourself eager for a fortifying cocktail.

Miriel, Pastor of Vows

An enormous turtle in a miter waits in the Church of Vows, selling his wares of Sorceries and Incantations. He never moves, neither to defend himself nor to abandon his post in the Church of Vows—a rare constant in the volatile Lands Between. A gentle companion and teacher, his drink is a moment of comfort for the Tarnished.

YIELD: 1 COCKTAIL

2 ounces Irish whiskey

½ ounce green chartreuse

½ ounce St-Germain elderflower liqueur

¼ ounce pineapple juice

1 bar spoon rich simple syrup (see box on page 18)

2 dashes aromatic bitters

1 pineapple frond, for garnish

Combine the whiskey, chartreuse, elder-flower liqueur, pineapple juice, simple syrup, and bitters in a mixing glass, then top with ice. Stir until chilled, 20 seconds, then strain into a stemmed cocktail glass. Garnish with the pineapple frond.

MMORPGS

A variation on the role-playing game, MMORPGs expand the community and the gameplay online. These massively multiplayer online role-playing games offer plenty of quests and player-versus-environment challenges, with the addition of player-versus-player capabilities: to both collaborate and compete. Some enemies will never be defeated alone, and sometimes more gear will turn up for certain players than they need and others not at all. With an MMORPG, there is always a chance to build a community through shared gameplay and synchronous enjoyment.

World of Warcraft

The most popular subscription MMORPG, *World of Warcraft* puts players in a fantasy world of monsters, dungeons, and quests. Joining the Alliance or the Horde, the world of Azeroth is your oyster. Quest chains build stories both large and small and with nine major expansions, the game is still vital, fresh, and exciting twenty years after its debut. A free-to-play version is available to try, raising characters to level 20 and offering a taste of the magic found in the full game.

The Lich King

One of the most iconic villains in the world of Azeroth, the Lich King sits atop his frozen throne, commanding the undead to do his bidding. Once a commander of the Burning Legion, wreathed in green flame, he betrayed his creator and claimed his own power. At the cocktail party, all must serve the one . . . true . . . king.

YIELD: 1 COCKTAIL

1 teaspoon kosher salt, for rimming

1½ ounces vodka

1 ounce cranberry juice

½ ounce Midori

¼ ounce Ginger Syrup (page 21)

1 bar spoon Hot Chili Tincture (page 22)

Rim the edge of your glass with kosher salt (see box on page 40). Combine the vodka, cranberry juice, Midori, ginger syrup, and chili tincture in a shaker, along with crushed ice. Shake for 10 seconds, then pour into a double old-fashioned glass over fresh crushed ice.

RuneScape

The largest and most updated free MMORPG, *RuneScape* has been drawing players into an open fantasy world since 2001. A balance of crafting skills and combat allows players an exciting range of adventures and quests, with no obligation to follow a specific story beyond the whims of accepting quests. The varying graphics of the game give *RuneScape* an instantly recognizable aesthetic that can be enjoyed on computers of all graphics power. An old-school RPG with enduring appeal, this game is a true classic of the genre.

Wizard Blizzard

A staple of gnome cooking, the Wizard Blizzard is a tropical treat that boosts strength, but at the cost of attack power. It might look like a strange mix, but it's a delicious treat with just a hint of juniper.

YIELD: 1 COCKTAIL

1 ounce vodka

½ ounce gin

½ ounce fresh lime juice

½ ounce fresh lemon juice

½ ounce fresh orange juice

½ ounce pineapple juice

1 lime wheel, for garnish

1 pineapple chunk, for garnish

Combine the vodka, gin, and juices in a shaker, then top with ice. Shake for 15 seconds, until chilled, then strain the liquid into the small tin. Discard the ice and shake for another 15 seconds (reverse dry shake—see box on page 73). Strain into an old-fashioned glass and garnish with the lime wheel and pineapple chunk.

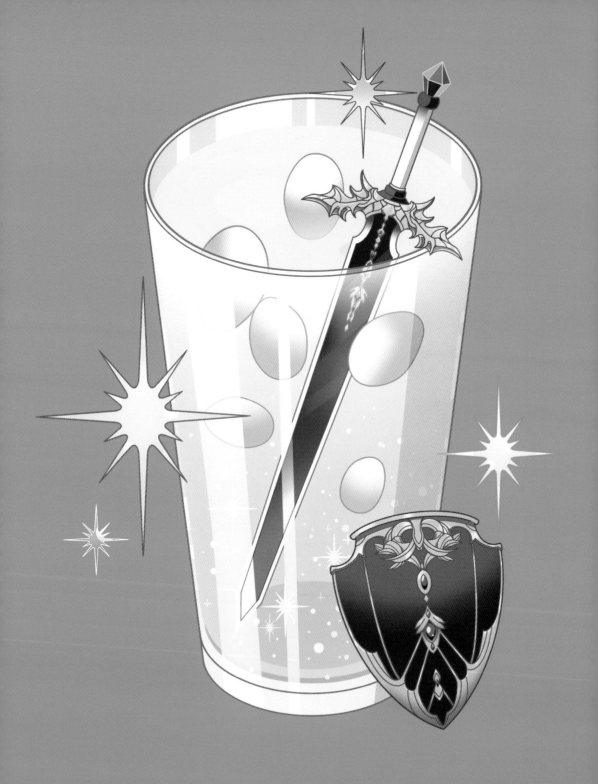

Final Fantasy XIV

This MMORPG in the Final Fantasy series from Square Enix debuted in 2013, but with four major expansions since then, it remains fresh and innovative more than a decade later. Replacing an earlier 2010 version of the game, *Final Fantasy XIV* has soared to become the most profitable entry in the series to date. Explore Hydaelyn in the early days of the Seventh Astral Era, a world on the mend, a world in need of heroes. With the option to play in PvE challenges and an exciting variety of PvP modes, this game offers a rich and novel experience for longtime series fans and MMORPG enthusiasts alike.

Ether

We've all been there: you're flying through a quest and feeling great, until you suddenly realize that last instance ate up the last of your mana . . . and it's *always* right when you're about to get hit with another wave of monsters. That's when you reach for your ether! Restore your energy and get back to kicking butt. In the real world, we all wake up a little slow some mornings and need a quick recovery. This drink is the perfect way to restart after a late night, whether you had a cocktail party or just needed to get that last side quest completed.

YIELD: 1 MOCKTAIL

12 ounces iced green tea

¾ ounce honey syrup (see page 18)

¾ ounce fresh lemon juice

1 Nuun citrus electrolyte tablet

Combine the iced tea, honey syrup, and lemon juice in a pint glass over crushed ice. Drop in the citrus tablet—this flavor works best here, but follow your bliss—and watch that golden fizz. Drink, recover, and enjoy.

BAR BYTES: USING TEA IN MOCKTAILS

When brewing tea for mocktails, brew it stronger than you would to drink on its own. You want the tea to be able to hold its own alongside the other ingredients in the drink.

Destiny

A popular online-only, multiplayer, first-person shooter, *Destiny* has been transporting players across the galaxy since its release in 2014. Since then, Guardians have explored the game's science fantasy mythos and defended the Earth from alien threats and the all-consuming Darkness in player-versus-environment and player-versus-player missions. With more than twelve expansions and a large cast of factions and NPCs to interact with, *Destiny* has plenty of reasons to keep players coming back to defend humanity against the Darkness.

The Ghost

The Guardian's companion and partner, the feisty floating robot is a source of comfort, information, and support. This bubbly, refreshing highball will float alongside you, just like your little friend.

YIELD: 1 COCKTAIL

1½ ounces vodka

¾ ounce lime cordial (see page 24)

½ ounce Midori

2 to 4 dashes grapefruit bitters

Lemon-lime soda

1 lime wheel, for garnish

Combine the vodka, lime cordial, Midori, and bitters in a shaker, then top with ice. Shake for 15 seconds, until frosty, then strain into a highball glass over fresh ice. Top with lemon-lime soda and garnish with the lime wheel.

ACTION-ADVENTURE AND STEALTH

Physical challenges and puzzles combine in these fast-paced games. You'll need to keep your mind sharp and your fingers ready for action as you delve through hidden tombs, infiltrate mansions and military facilities, or swing from building to building. Whether the emphasis is on combat or stealth, the action-adventure game keeps things moving with compelling levels, missions, and equipment. Sometimes, it's enough just to survive . . .

Metal Gear Solid

Regarded by many as one of the greatest video games of all time, 1987's *Metal Gear* introduced gamers to Solid Snake, a special forces operator tasked with neutralizing a terrorist attack from the renegade FOXHOUND unit. The game was a pioneer in the stealth genre and widely celebrated for the deliberation of gameplay, the extended cinematic quality of the game, and the series' cutscenes. With nearly a dozen main sequence games and almost as many spinoffs and remakes, this series is as vital today as it was when it premiered.

Liquid Snake

Solid Snake's twin brother and the primary antagonist in *Metal Gear Solid*, Liquid Snake was introduced in 1998. In *Metal Gear Solid V: The Phantom Pain*, a younger Liquid Snake appears as a child mercenary codenamed White Mamba. Resentful of the protagonist's favor with their "father," Liquid Snake is a commanding villain committed to proving his own superiority. His namesake drink is sharp and assertive, with a spiced note of darkness intermingled with the pale fizz of the other flavors.

YIELD: 1 COCKTAIL

1½ ounces vodka

1 ounce fresh lemon juice

½ ounce ouzo

½ ounce Orgeat (page 23)

2 dashes aromatic bitters

Seltzer

1 lemon peel, for garnish

Combine the vodka, lemon juice, ouzo, orgeat, and bitters in a shaker, then add ice. Shake for 15 seconds, until frosty, then strain into a highball glass over fresh ice. Top with seltzer and garnish with a snake peel (see box).

Garnish Game: Snake Peel

This works best with a lemon, which has the perfect balance of size and thickness of skin, but you can also do it with an orange or grapefruit. (Limes are often too small and with skins too thin for a long wide twist like the snake.) Using a vegetable peeler, paring knife, or twist peeler, cut a wide twist from your fruit. Cut into the fruit with the twist peeler and rotate the fruit away from you, cutting into the peel and working your way around the fruit. Make the twist as long as you can. When you have finished the twist, use a paring knife to even up the sides and cut one end into a narrow point for the tail. At the other end, cut a diamond-shaped head. If you're especially ambitious, you can try cutting out a forked tongue as well. For the eyes, either poke two small holes or add two cloves to the head.

Tomb Raider

The 1996 release of *Tomb Raider* introduced gamers to a world of ruined temples, hidden treasures, puzzles, and battles, all anchored by a daring heroine and a winking nod to the aesthetics of antiquity. Lara Croft, the one and only Tomb Raider, is one of the most recognizable characters in video games, with her dual pistols, khaki shorts, blue-gray tank top, and long brunette braid. An archeologist-adventurer in the tradition of Indiana Jones and Allan Quatermain, Lara Croft works her way through physics-based puzzles, traps, environmental hazards, and wicked henchmen in the pursuit of lost treasures. With a dozen games in the main series and nearly as many spinoffs, *Tomb Raider* is a thrilling adventure not to be missed.

Scion Sipper

There are four major settings for the original *Tomb Raider*—Peru, Greece, and Egypt—each of which hides a piece of the mysterious Scion and its eventual power to restore the lost continent of Atlantis. Our highball takes inspiration from all four of these locations (you'll permit us some license on the fictional island of Atlantis) for a refreshing highball redolent with spices. Pisco, Peruvian brandy, can be difficult to find, but is well worth the effort.

YIELD: 1 COCKTAIL

1½ ounces pisco

1 ounce fresh lime juice

½ ounce ouzo

2 to 4 dashes cardamom bitters

Tonic water

Combine the pisco, lime juice, ouzo, and bitters in a shaker, then top with ice. Shake for 15 seconds, until frosty, then strain into a highball glass over fresh ice. Top with tonic water and relax after making your way through a long-forgotten ruin.

Hitman

A series of stealth games with eight mainline titles released since 2000, the Hitman franchise casts the player as a contract killer. Agent 47 is a globe-trotting assassin tasked with the elimination of various targets by the International Contract Agency. The sandbox world makes it easy to explore different techniques for accomplishing the contract killing, but emphasis is always on stealth, using disguises to enter restricted areas without being caught, and a successful escape. In 2016, the series had a soft reboot with a new trilogy, now available as an omnibus *Hitman: World of Assassination*, exploring the complete character arc of this well-known assassin even though names are friends that he doesn't need.

Agent 47

The bald Agent 47 is discreet, neutral in appearance, and almost mannequin-like: a blank slate for the player and for the various techniques of stealth and assassination employed during a game. When not employing a disguise, he typically dresses in an understated black suit, not formal but hardly casual. His work puts him in the company of the rich, powerful, and criminal, so this drink is right at home at a swanky cocktail party. In the ballroom or aboard a yacht, this riff on the classic champagne cocktail is sure to please. You'll want to be discreet making these at a party to celebrate the spirit of the game. Set yourself the challenge of serving champagne and seeing how many friends' drinks you can doctor before you're detected!

YIELD: 1 COCKTAIL

1 sugar cube

2 to 4 dashes black walnut bitters

6 ounces sparkling wine

On a small plate, douse your sugar cube with the bitters. With a pair of tongs, discreetly drop the prepared sugar cube into a glass of sparkling wine. Be prepared to make an escape while your target enjoys their cocktail.

+1 Nonalcoholic: Substitute sparkling grape juice or sparkling apple cider for the wine. Bitters do not add a measurable quantity of alcohol to a drink, but for a totally alcohol-free option, consider a glycerin-based bitters, like El Guapo Chicory Pecan Bitters.

BAR BYTES: FIZZ

Why add a sugar cube to champagne? The answer is bubbles. People love the fizz of sparkling wine—that's why we order it, that's why it's celebratory. And a sugar cube (or a raisin, in some cases) helps generate a fizzier, more festive glass of bubbly. With more surface area for the wine to interact with, more tiny bubbles are generated and a more effervescent cocktail with them. Just be sure not to sip too much!

Grand Theft Auto

A defining series for many gamers in the early 2000s, this action-adventure places you behind the wheel as you rise through the criminal underworld of Liberty City, San Andreas, or Vice City. An open world offers plenty of opportunities for exploration and innovative side enterprises, while the focus of the main story remains on auto theft, driving, and shooting. Full immersion from in-world radio stations and recognizable parodies gives a layer of realism to the bombastic glory of criminal indulgence.

High-Octane Highball

Don't drink and drive! Unless you're playing an action-adventure crime game from the comfort of your own home. You might not play as well after this refreshing high-heat cocktail, but you'll be ready to put rubber to the road in your life of crime. Whether you're cruising the beaches of Vice City or rolling through the Los Santos hills, a good drink is essential.

YIELD: 1 COCKTAIL

2 ounces vodka

1 ounce fresh grapefruit juice

½ ounce fresh lime juice

½ ounce Orgeat (page 23)

¼ ounce Hot Chili Tincture (page 22)

Seltzer

1 lime wheel, for garnish

Combine the vodka, grapefruit juice, lime juice, orgeat, and chili tincture in a shaker, then top with ice. Shake until chilled and frosty, then strain into a highball glass over fresh ice. Top with seltzer and garnish with the lime wheel.

Assassin's Creed

The Assassin's Creed franchise is a cross-genre action-adventure series combining stealth, combat, and open-world exploration with an intertwined alternative reality informed by real history and archeology as much as speculative elements. A battle between freedom and control across more than a dozen games since 2007 has brought players from early modern Italian city-states to pirate ships in the Caribbean to the streets of ancient Alexandria and beyond.

Enkidu Cooler

Assassin's Creed: Mirage, the newest game in the well-known franchise series, inspired this mocktail with its Middle Eastern flavors and bright, fruit-forward shrubs. Set in medieval Baghdad, the game follows Basim, a member of the Order of Assassins, as he comes into his own after previously appearing in 2020's Assassin's Creed: Valhalla. As he sneaks through the streets of Baghdad in the Islamic Golden Age, he is aided by an animal companion, the eastern imperial eagle, Enkidu. A more intimate game than its predecessors, Mirage elevates and engages in the immersive world of the medieval Middle East.

YIELD: 1 MOCKTAIL

1½ ounces Melon Shrub (page 20)

¾ ounce fresh lemon juice

½ ounce honey syrup (see page 18)

2 to 4 dashes aromatic bitters

Ginger beer

1 piece candied ginger

Combine the shrub, lemon juice, honey syrup, and bitters in a shaker, then top with ice. Shake until chilled and frosty, then strain into a highball glass over fresh crushed ice. Top with ginger beer and garnish with the candied ginger.

BAR BYTES: SHRUBS

From the Arabic al sharab, shrubs are fruit syrups made with vinegar, and are a great ingredient for both cocktails and mocktails. See page 20 for recipes.

Dishonored

A grimy steampunk city beckons in the 2012 action-adventure game *Dishonored*. A disgraced bodyguard works as an assassin to seek his revenge on the villains who plotted against him and his murdered empress. Stealth and combat combine in this game, and for the determined and sneaky player, it is possible to complete all missions nonlethally. Two sequels appeared in 2016 and 2017, and then 2021 saw the release of a spinoff, *Deathloop*, set centuries after the events of the *Dishonored* trilogy. You'll have a whale of a time with this series!

Lady Boyle's Last Party Punch

Dishonored draws on the aesthetics of the nineteenth century, a grimy Victorian mire, amid whale oil and shining brass. A masquerade ball needs a proper punch, and the eighteenth and nineteenth centuries were the golden age for this communal drink. This classic punch recipe hearkens to days of polite whispers, top hats, and deadly secrets, perfect for your next party, which will hopefully be assassin-free.

YIELD: 20 COCKTAILS

8 lemons

1½ cups sugar

3 cups iced black tea

2 cups brandy

1 cup apple brandy

1 cup Irish whiskey

1 (750 mL) bottle sparkling wine

Alternative: If you don't feel like making the oleo-saccharum for this punch, substitute 1½ cups lemon cordial (see page 24). To make the punch, continue to include the fresh lemon juice, but balance with ⅓ cup rich simple syrup.

Peel 4 of the lemons—ensuring you have nice big strips of the peel—and place the strips in the bottom of your punch bowl. Cover the peels with the sugar and leave them to sit for 2 hours to create an oleo-saccharum, a sugar oil. Stir to help dissolve the sugar in the extracted oils, then remove the lemon peels and either discard or save to use as a garnish. Juice all the lemons over the sugar and stir to combine. Add the iced tea, brandy, apple brandy, and whiskey and stir to combine. Taste as you mix—you may wish to add a splash of rich simple syrup or brightening lemon juice to suit your palate. Allow to sit until party time, but if the wait will be longer than 4 hours, cover and store in the fridge.

When your first guest arrives, add a large block of ice (see box on page 154) and top with the sparkling wine. Ladle into stemmed cocktail glasses or punch cups.

Press Start to Play!

The assassin is a recurring player character in many games, given the emphasis on stealth, physicality, and single-player point of view. Even though the characters and their adventures may be lonely, it's nice to celebrate our favorite gaming assassins with friends and an assassin-themed party!

Open the evening with a sparkling Agent 47 (page 119) or an Enkidu Cooler (page 121). Mix up a batch of Lady Boyle's Last Party Punch (page 122) to keep the crowd going between turns, and maybe throw in a few rounds of Impostor Shots (page 163). When you are ready to save the game and chill, shake up a vodka martini à la James Bond (page 135), or a nightcap of B. J. Blazkowicz (page 134) will have you ready for bed and quite contented.

Red Dead Redemption 2

The 2018 sequel to 2010's *Red Dead Redemption*, itself a follow-up to *Red Dead Revolver*, *Red Dead Redemption 2* is a Western-themed action-adventure game where you are completely in control of who you want to be and where you want to go. We've seen a lot of action-adventure assassins, but here you step into the boots of an outlaw in the waning days of the Wild West at the turn of the twentieth century. An open world gives lots to explore and a reputation system ensures that you control whether you're the hero or the villain of the West. The regions of this alternative United States are fictional but recognizable, a West that is tied to American history but still open enough for new events and unfamiliar history. The game is unpredictable and wide-ranging, yet still governed by a powerful narrative and strong characterization.

Boadicea's Neck

A playful take on a classic American mocktail, the Horse's Neck, our *Red Dead Redemption* drink wouldn't be complete without something red! Peychaud's bitters are a classic aromatic bitters with anise and rosehip flavors. Strongly associated with the southeastern United States and especially New Orleans, Peychaud's is the perfect bottle to have on hand when you're exploring Lemoyne astride your trusty steed.

YIELD: 1 MOCKTAIL

6 to 8 fresh mint leaves, plus 1 mint sprig for garnish

1 ounce lemon cordial (see page 24)

½ ounce mint simple syrup (see page 18)

4 to 6 dashes Peychaud's bitters

Seltzer

1 lemon twist (see box on page 79), for garnish

Gently muddle the mint leaves in the bottom of a highball glass. Add the lemon cordial, mint syrup, bitters, and ice. Top with seltzer and stir to combine. Garnish with a long twist of lemon, curled around the interior of your highball glass, and a sprig of mint.

+1 Alcohol: Add 1 ounce Guarma Rum, Gin, Fine Brandy, or Kentucky Bourbon. Maybe skip the Saloon Whiskey—we're not sure what's in it.

BAR BYTES: THE HORSE AND THE MULE

When you add alcohol to a Horse's Neck, you make it a mule or a buck. Like the famous Moscow Mule, it's a highball with a kick!

Spider-Man

The 2018 release of *Spider-Man* put players in control of Marvel's most beloved hero as he battles crime across Manhattan with a wide cast drawn from decades of Spider-Man lore. Villains, allies, friends, and foes all converge on Peter Parker. Miles Morales also appears, and takes on a larger role in the sequel game *Spider-Man 2*, which also introduces the corrupting Venom symbiote. The open world of Manhattan is drawn from life and the environmental storytelling is a true delight. For fans seeking an innovative combat system and compelling heroic story, this is a landmark title.

The Spectacular Spider-Sour

The New York Sour, with its distinctive red wine float, is one of the most iconic variations on the classic whiskey sour. The red wine does more than serve as an aesthetic garnish; it adds a fruity depth and warming spice to the bright zing of the sour. To pay homage to Spider-Man's classic blue and red costume, we have brought an extra burst of citrus to our sour with blue curaçao. Look for a dry red wine here, like a shiraz. This is a drink that will have you ready to swing between skyscrapers alongside your favorite webslinger.

YIELD: 1 COCKTAIL

1½ ounces bourbon whiskey

¾ ounce fresh lemon juice

½ ounce blue curaçao

¼ ounce rich simple syrup (see box on page 18)

½ ounce dry red wine

Combine the bourbon, lemon juice, curaçao, and simple syrup in a shaker, then top with ice. Shake for 15 seconds, then strain into a stemmed cocktail glass. Float the red wine on top (see box) and enjoy.

Garnish Game: Floats

A float is a layering of another liquid on top of the main body of your cocktail or mocktail. Less dense liquids will remain largely separated and slowly seep into the body of the drink, changing the experience over the course of sipping and creating a dramatic garnish. To do a float, place the edge of your bar spoon on the inner rim of the glass, just above the surface of the drink. Pour the float liquid over the top of your drink and enjoy. This technique is tricky, so practice before you try this for a party!

The Last of Us

Explore the broken world amid the ravages of an apocalyptic disaster. Fungal monstrosities walk the land as Joel and Ellie seek a cure to the mutant plague. Stealth and combat combine with a killer story and poignant characterization. A sense of vulnerability and a deep empathy pervade the game, with the reminder that the enemies are victims first, and the fight is for humanity's survival. This is a gut-wrenching game and a testament to the storytelling capabilities of the medium married to top-quality gameplay.

SurRYEvor

Canned goods and preserved food offer health and wellness, but you can't afford to be too picky or precise. The end of the world means getting back to basics. This recipe swaps out heavy cream for shelf-stable evaporated milk, and it'll be a dark day indeed when we're denied our whiskey and oats.

YIELD: 1 COCKTAIL

1 ounce rye whiskey

1 ounce evaporated milk

½ ounce oat syrup (see page 18)

½ ounce cinnamon syrup (see page 18)

2 to 4 dashes aromatic bitters

¼ teaspoon ground cinnamon, for garnish

Combine the rye, evaporated milk, syrups, and bitters in a shaker, then top with ice. Shake for 15 seconds, until chilled, then strain the liquid into the small tin. Discard the ice and shake for another 15 seconds (reverse dry shake—see box on page 73). Strain into an old-fashioned glass and garnish with a sprinkle of cinnamon.

Bloated Mushrooms

The most dangerous stage of the cordyceps infection is the Bloater. Coated with fungal armor and extremely aggressive, these enemies are incredibly difficult to eliminate. Fortunately, the mushrooms at the grocery are much more tender. Try this appetizer at your next cocktail party.

YIELD: 12 STUFFED MUSHROOMS

2 tablespoons unsalted butter, divided

1 small onion, minced

2 garlic cloves, minced

1 pound button mushrooms

1 large egg

8 ounces goat cheese

½ cup bread crumbs

1½ teaspoons salt

1 teaspoon black pepper

Seasonings

Dash brandy or water

½ cup shredded cheddar cheese

Hot tip: Remember, it's an apocalypse out there; use the seasonings you have on hand. I like dried marjoram, basil, and thyme for a more herbal approach. Or try cayenne pepper, ground mustard, and white pepper for a bit more of a kick.

Heat 1 tablespoon of the butter in a small saucepan over medium heat. Add the onion and garlic and sauté until softened, 5 to 7 minutes.

Remove the stems from the mushrooms and save the 12 largest caps. Chop the remaining mushroom caps and stems, then add them to the pan with the onion and garlic. Sauté for 20 minutes, until the mushrooms are soft and golden brown.

Meanwhile, preheat the oven to 350 degrees F. Line a 9-inch baking pan with aluminum foil.

Beat the egg in a large bowl. Add the goat cheese, bread crumbs, salt, pepper, and seasonings and mix well.

When the mushrooms are done, deglaze the pan with a splash of brandy and scrape up the browned bits. Transfer the mushrooms to the goat cheese mixture and stir to combine. Spoon the filling mixture into the reserved mushroom caps, then top with the cheddar cheese.

Melt the remaining 1 tablespoon butter and brush the tops of the stuffed mushrooms. Place the stuffed mushrooms in the prepared pan and bake for 20 minutes, or until the cheese is bubbly. Serve hot.

Death Stranding

From action-adventure maestro Hideo Kojima, the mind behind *Metal Gear* (see page 116), came 2019's *Death Stranding*. Play as courier Sam Bridges in a world wracked by a cataclysm that blurs the lines between the living and the dead, between rapid entropy and the needs of connection. Complete deliveries and make sense of the open world. This is a game of connection and distance: you can find the lost cargo of other players but never encounter those players. Atmospheric and engaging, the promise of a sequel suggests a new subgenre in the world of action-adventure games is due to emerge.

Timefall Fizz

Timefall is one of the key dangers of the game, a deleterious precipitation that wears away at every protection: entropy by way of acid rain. This weighty fizz has softer foam than one made with egg white, and its dark bubbles demand a quick sip.

YIELD: 1 COCKTAIL

1 teaspoon demerara sugar, for rimming

1½ ounces brandy

½ ounce lime cordial (see page 24)

½ ounce cranberry juice

½ ounce blue curaçao

¼ ounce saline solution (see box on page 91)

1 bar spoon whole milk powder

2 ounces seltzer

Rim the edge of a highball glass with demerara sugar (see box on page 40). Combine the brandy, lime cordial, cranberry juice, curaçao, saline, and milk powder in a shaker. Stir to combine, then dry shake for 15 seconds. Add ice and shake for another 15 seconds. Double-strain into a highball glass and top with seltzer.

SHOOTERS

Whether you're looking through the eyes of your character or down from above, the shooter genre is ready to pit you against foes with all the weapons you need. The emphasis is on combat, with a variety of tools to accomplish each mission. You may be battling Nazis, aliens, mutants, or monsters, but you can be sure that the shooter genre will provide endless challenges for single-player action or multiplayer madness.

Wolfenstein

Since 1981, the Wolfenstein series has seen several iterations, but one goal remains the same: battling Nazis and the Axis powers. From the series' origins as World War II adventure stealth to the introduction of Nazi fascination with the occult and a battle against supernatural entities and over paranormal artifacts, to the alternative history where the Nazis win the war and must be resisted across the world, Wolfenstein stays fresh and exciting through the generations. The first game, *Castle Wolfenstein*, was an early title in the stealth genre, but the series has come into its own as first-person shooters, starting with *Wolfenstein 3D*, which also introduced the series' occult elements. The first-person shooter genre owes much of its early popularity to the innovations of *Wolfenstein 3D*.

B. J. Blazkowicz

The hero of the Wolfenstein series, B. J. Blazkowicz is an agent of the Office of Secret Actions tasked with thwarting the secret projects of the Nazis. A notorious skeptic, he nevertheless battles the occult, putting his faith in lead and gunsmoke. The Milwaukee-born son of Polish immigrants, he inspired this riff on a Wisconsin Old-Fashioned.

YIELD: 1 COCKTAIL

2 ounces brandy

½ ounce Islay Scotch whisky

½ ounce lapsang souchong syrup
(see "tea syrup" on page 18)

1 to 3 dashes aromatic bitters, preferably
18.21 Havana & Hide

1 flamed orange peel (see box),
for garnish

Combine the brandy, whisky, tea syrup, and bitters in a rocks glass over a large ice cube and stir to combine. Garnish with a flamed orange peel.

Garnish Game: Flaming an Orange Peel

Peel your citrus with a Y-peeler, cutting a wide swath. Light a match. Hold the match in one hand and the peel in the other over the surface of your glass. Pinch the peel to express the orange oils and watch those sparks dance on the surface of your cocktail.

GoldenEye 007

Released two years after the film *GoldenEye*, in 1997, *GoldenEye 007* put gamers in control of literature and film's best-known spy: James Bond. While the first-person shooter game is primarily single player, this game was well known for its multiplayer mode, which allows up to four players to participate in deathmatch games. *GoldenEye 007* paved the way for later console-based first-person shooters, and while the look and sound of the game are very much of their era, gameplay continues to engage and delight gamers of all ages. The game was remade in 2010 for the Nintendo DS and subsequently ported to other consoles of early 2010s. Perhaps someday soon, *GoldenEye 007* will capture the minds of a new generation of gamers on a whole new platform . . . a classic is a classic for a reason.

James Bond's Martini

"Vodka martini, shaken not stirred." There is hardly a more iconic cocktail order in the world, and the dry martini ordered by James Bond has cemented the public consciousness of the drink for more than sixty years. And yet . . . it is hardly a traditional martini. In fact, in the original James Bond novel, *Casino Royale*, Ian Fleming decided to have his character order a martini in a nontraditional fashion—made with vodka instead of gin, exceptionally dry, and stirred rather than shaken—to show the then-novice spy as somewhat out of place in the high circles his mission took him on. Little did he know that the debonair character would dominate the latter half of the twentieth century and reshape generations of martini orders. Of course, there's no wrong way to have a martini, wet or dry, shaken or stirred, but for a spy on the go, the shaken martini is perfect for a life of adventure.

YIELD: 1 COCKTAIL

2½ ounces vodka, preferably Stoli

½ ounce dry vermouth

1 lemon twist (see box on page 79) or olive, for garnish

Combine the vodka and vermouth in a shaker, then top with ice. Shake vigorously until chilled, then strain into a stemmed cocktail glass. Garnish with the lemon twist or olive.

Easter Egg

Cortana, the AI in the Halo series, lent her name to the Microsoft virtual assistant.

Halo

Dangers abound in the twenty-sixth century, but super soldier Master Chief is up to the challenge in this landmark shooter title. Explore the titular Halo, a mysterious artificial ringworld, with your plasma weapons and the aid of AI Cortana. Battle your way through the forces of the Covenant and the Flood as you seek to understand the facility's purpose and the threat it poses to humankind. And look forward to numerous expansions of the franchise and sequel games! It was the ubiquitous green branding of *Halo* that helped cement the game and series as *the* flagship title for the Xbox console, proving Microsoft was a contender on the console market.

Flood Shot

Infectious alien life-forms that consume sentient matter, the Flood are a dangerous threat in the world of *Halo*. Their parasitism ensures near endless variability, and the threat of a communal Gravemind lurks at the edge of conjoined consciousness. Share this shot with your friends and be as one.

YIELD: 1 SHOT

½ ounce absinthe

½ ounce crème de menthe

½ ounce Midori

1 bar spoon blue curaçao

¼ ounce heavy cream

Build your drink in a shot glass, starting with the absinthe, then the crème de menthe, Midori, and blue curaçao. Layer the heavy cream on top. Knock back and kick some alien ass.

Hot tip: Mix up a large batch of all the ingredients except the heavy cream, and measure out 1½ ounces for each guest at your party. That way you aren't spending all evening building. The heavy cream gives the drink its signature effect, so be sure to save that for when it's time to enjoy your shots.

BAR BYTES: ABSINTHE LOUCHE AND THE OUZO EFFECT

If you have ever enjoyed absinthe or ouzo, you will have noticed that the clear liquid turns a milky white or green when you add water. This is called the ouzo effect, or louche. It is a phenomenon that occurs in anise-based spirits and liqueurs as essential oils such as anise camphor emulsify in the water. It is an effect that feels like magic every time and a great way to determine whether your spirit is made with genuine anise compounds.

Call of Duty: Modern Warfare

The first three games in the Call of Duty franchise, released between 2003 and 2006, are first-person shooters set during World War II, a legacy that has been revisited and revived in later titles, but it is the *Modern Warfare* timeline that looms large over the series. Missions are set against the anxieties of the twenty-first century, and modern weapons follow deployments across the Middle East, eastern Europe, and Russia. Multiple game modes, from a single-player campaign to co-op survival, give players lots of options for replayability. More than 400 million copies of the series' nineteen games have sold, making Call of Duty the most successful first-person shooter series in the world.

Bravo Spritz

For queen and country. Sergeant (later Captain) John "Soap" MacTavish, a member of team Bravo Six, is a British Special Air Serviceman and a main character in the Modern Warfare series. Alongside Captain John Price, Sergeant Wallcroft, Private Griffen, and Gaz (rank unknown), MacTavish is playable in parts of *Modern Warfare 1, 2*, and *3*, and otherwise an NPC. A strong support for Captain John Price, MacTavish served in the Second Russian Civil War and World War III. Our drink is strong and sharp with a bittersweet heat.

YIELD: 1 COCKTAIL

1½ ounces blended Scotch whisky

¾ ounce dry vermouth

½ ounce cinnamon syrup (see page 18)

¼ ounce Campari

1 bar spoon Hot Chili Tincture (page 22)

Ginger beer

2 to 4 dashes aromatic bitters

Combine the whisky, vermouth, syrup, Campari, and chili tincture in a mixing glass, then top with ice. Stir for 20 seconds, then strain into a highball glass over fresh ice. Top with ginger beer and "crown" with bitters by dashing over the top of the cocktail.

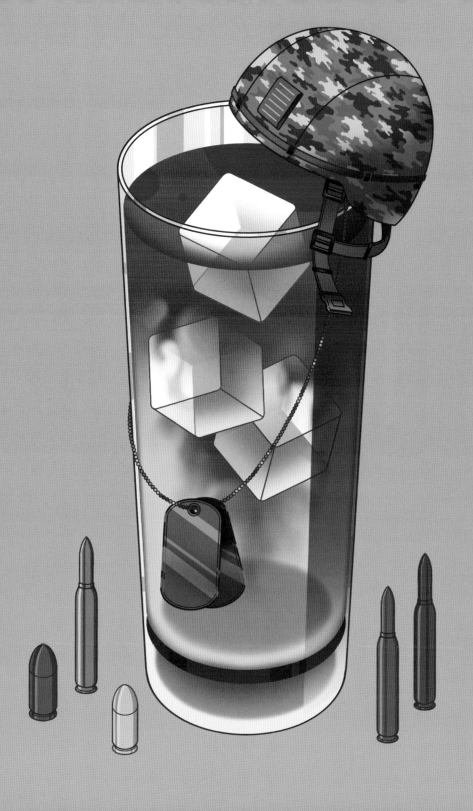

BioShock

Deep beneath the sea lies the city of Rapture, a utopian dream turned to a hyper-imbalanced powder keg of tensions between titans of industry and Jack, the sole survivor of a mid-Atlantic plane crash. The 2007 first-person shooter explores the conflicting motives of free will and power, altruism, and exploitation. With a gleaming art deco environment beneath the green-black waters, the game and its sequels delight with their thoughtfulness, visual immersion, and exciting levels of stealth and combat.

Plasmid

Special serums that make use of gene modification to grant strange powers and fearsome mutations, Plasmids are an essential tool for Jack as he battles his way through Rapture, exploring gameplay styles beyond the capability of mere weapons. This cocktail can't grant mutagenic marvels, but it's delicious enough that you won't mind.

YIELD: 1 COCKTAIL

1¼ ounces brandy

¾ ounce Campari

½ ounce red wine syrup (see page 18)

¼ ounce Raspberry Liqueur (page 22)

2 to 4 dashes aromatic bitters

1 orange peel, for garnish

Combine the brandy, Campari, syrup, liqueur, and bitters in a mixing glass, then top with ice. Stir for 20 seconds, then strain into a stemmed cocktail glass. Garnish with an expressed orange peel (see box on page 43).

Arcadia Spinach-Artichoke Dip

The fifth level of *BioShock* takes place in Arcadia, the breadbasket of the city beneath the sea. A source of life and a tranquil haven, Rapture's Vacationland inspired this crowd-pleasing party snack.

YIELD: 6 SERVINGS

1 (8-ounce) package cream cheese

1 (12-ounce) can quartered artichoke hearts, drained

1 (10-ounce) bag frozen spinach, thawed and squeezed dry

1 cup shredded mozzarella cheese, divided

½ cup grated Parmesan cheese

½ cup sour cream

1 tablespoon fresh lemon juice

1 teaspoon salt

½ teaspoon black pepper

½ teaspoon garlic powder

½ teaspoon cayenne pepper

Pita chips, crackers, or tortilla chips, for serving

Preheat the oven to 375 degrees F. Combine the cream cheese, artichoke hearts, spinach, ½ cup of the mozzarella, the Parmesan, sour cream, lemon juice, salt, black pepper, garlic powder, and cayenne in a large bowl. Mix well. Spread the mixture into a 9-inch baking pan. Bake for 20 minutes. Top with the remaining ½ cup mozzarella cheese and bake for another 10 minutes. Turn on the broiler and broil for 3 minutes, until golden-brown on top. Serve with your favorite dippers.

Hot tip: You can also make this spinach and artichoke dip in a slow cooker, keeping it warm all evening long. Just remember that it will be harder to get that bubbling crust of melty cheese on top!

Resident Evil Village

2021's *Resident Evil Village* is an action-adventure game in the popular Resident Evil survival horror franchise. With more emphasis on combat than other games in the franchise, *Resident Evil Village* is a sequel to 2017's *Resident Evil 7: Biohazard*, and players control Ethan Winters as he battles werewolf-like mutants and other horrifying dangers. Can you sneak, scavenge, and survive long enough to locate Ethan's missing daughter and escape from this haunted village and Mother Miranda?

Lady Dimitrescu Fizz

Inspired by the giant vampiresque aristocrat, Lady Dimitrescu is one of the lords of the village who must be defeated and a standout, fan-favorite character. With her powerful, authoritative personality, signature long white dress, and broad sweeping hat, she is not the main villain, but her distinctive appearance captured the hearts of gamers and artists across the internet. Her drink is a shaken fizz with rich floral depth, as blue-blooded as they come. This is a tall drink for a tall lady.

YIELD: 1 COCKTAIL

1 small rosemary sprig

1½ ounces gin

¾ ounce lime cordial (see page 24)

½ ounce crème de menthe

¼ ounce crème de violette

¼ ounce Simple Syrup (page 17)

1 large egg white (see box)

1 (12-ounce can) seltzer

Gently muddle the rosemary sprig in the bottom of the shaker, then add the gin, lime cordial, crème de menthe, crème de violette, simple syrup, and egg white. Dry shake for 30 seconds. Add 2 ice cubes and shake until they are broken up and melted, about 20 seconds. Double-strain into a highball glass and top with the seltzer. Be careful not to pour too quickly, as the foam will extend beyond the top of the glass.

BAR BYTES: USING EGG WHITE IN COCKTAILS

Egg white is a classic ingredient in cocktails, in shaken sours and especially in effervescent fizzes. The egg adds texture to the drink, emulsifying and forming a light but sturdy foam as the drink is shaken. The alcohol and citrus eliminates much of the risk of salmonella, but if you are uncomfortable using egg white in your fizzes, replace with ½ ounce aquafaba (canned chickpea water), 1 bar spoon whole milk powder, or 6 to 8 dashes Fee Foam.

COMPETITIVE AND FIGHTING GAMES

Fighting games with hand-to-hand combat and special moves, sports games and racing simulators, battle royales and hero shooters—these games bring the spirit of competition to the fore. Whether you're playing against a game's AI, your friends and family, or a rival on the other side of the world, these games offer a thrilling matchup and battle for the ages. The vibrant esports community thrives in these games, but they bring just as much enjoyment to casual players as well. Continue?

Street Fighter

From arcade classic to multi-platform marvel, *Street Fighter* is an essential franchise in one-on-one combat. The original arcade game pitted Japanese martial artist Ryu against his American friend and rival Ken Masters, but it was *Street Fighter II* that really changed the game and the genre. Now nearly 100 characters are available to play, and the competitive gaming scene around the series thrives. Remember: your special moves and distinctive fighting style are the path to total victory.

Button Smash

Not all of us are good at fighting games. We don't remember our favorite character's special moves, we don't dodge or weave or strike with precision, we just press buttons and hope for the best. And that's OK! Competition is all well and good, but at the end of the day it's about having fun. The smash is one of those classic cocktail formats that is always frosty and refreshing, no matter the state of the match.

YIELD: 1 COCKTAIL

1 strawberry, quartered

2 blueberries

2 raspberries

2 blackberries

2 ounces bourbon whiskey

1 ounce lemon juice

½ ounce mint simple syrup (see page 18)

1 mint sprig, for garnish

Muddle the berries in the bottom of a shaker, then add the bourbon, lemon juice, mint syrup, and a scoop of crushed ice. Shake until frosty, 15 seconds, then pour into an old-fashioned glass over fresh crushed ice. Garnish with the mint sprig.

Mortal Kombat

One of the quintessential fighting games, the original *Mortal Kombat* debuted in 1992. Since then, the franchise has seen twenty-six main and spinoff games, creating a connected universe of unique thematic realms where you must defeat the greatest warrior in a martial arts tournament: the eponymous *Mortal Kombat*. The overarching plot looms over the principal fighting mechanic but does not overwhelm as six mainline games were released between 1992 and 2006. In 2011, a second game titled *Mortal Kombat* served as a soft reboot of the series, followed by two sequels that both received substantial DLCs. In 2023 the series was rebooted a second time with *Mortal Kombat 1*, a sequel to 2019's *Mortal Kombat 11*. There's a *Mortal Kombat* for each new generation, proving that there's always an appetite for fierce combat and bombastic gore. Finish them!

Finishing Move

If you play *Street Fighter* to win or lose, you play *Mortal Kombat* for that finishing move: the Fatality, the special move that your fighter has that will overwhelm your opponent and end the match. You cannot help but cringe and cheer as the brutal and gruesome Fatalities are played out in all their cinematic glory. This drink is a high-octane shot to get the party started. Or finished.

YIELD: 1 COCKTAIL

¾ ounce overproof rum

½ ounce amaretto

¼ ounce ouzo

1 bar spoon Grenadine (page 19)

Build your drink in the shot glass, starting with the rum and ending with the grenadine. Knock it back at a KO and get back to the match.

Wii Sports

2006's *Wii Sports* collected five popular sports—tennis, baseball, bowling, golf, and boxing—and paired them with the novel motion-sensing technology of the Wii remote. Now the actions of the player could be replicated in the game; though it limited and only mimicked the motions of each sport, it was pretty exciting. A flagship game for the Wii console system, *Wii Sports* is the best-selling Nintendo game of all time, surpassing even *Super Mario Bros.* A true delight to play with the whole family or against friends on a Friday night, *Wii Sports* is a video game with endless replayability and an enduring legacy.

Wii Tennis Cooler

A more intense variation of the Pong Punch (page 28), this mocktail will have you ready to bat the tennis ball back and forth across the virtual court all night long. A far cry from the focused joystick gameplay of *Pong*, *Wii Tennis* has its players standing, bringing the gentle clap and rapt attention of Wimbledon to the living room at home. You'll *love* it!

YIELD: 1 MOCKTAIL

4 ounces ginger beer

4 ounces pineapple juice

½ ounce fresh lime juice

½ ounce passion fruit syrup

2 to 4 dashes orange bitters

1 lime twist (see box on page 79), for garnish

Combine the ginger beer, juices, syrup, and bitters in a highball glass over ice and stir to combine. Garnish with the lime twist.

Gran Turismo

For more than a quarter century, driving enthusiasts have been turning to *Gran Turismo* to race high-end vehicles. Single-player and multiplayer modes offer a variety of options for players in this driving simulator that places an emphasis on realism. The physics are so accurate and precise that elite players have gone on to compete in professional real-life racing. For the casual player or automotive enthusiast, there is no better way to test-drive premium vehicles and compete on the world stage of racing.

Sardegna Simulator Spritz

A fictional circuit complex, the four Sardegna tracks offer a variety of road conditions from dirt tracks to sharp inclines. Along the shores of the Mediterranean, there's always a beautiful view and a challenging race. You need to keep your wits about you as you tear around the track, so this bittersweet spritz is totally alcohol free.

YIELD: 1 MOCKTAIL

1 ounce white grape juice

1 ounce Giffard aperitif syrup

½ ounce Ginger Syrup (page 21)

2 to 4 dashes orange bitters

2 ounces sparkling apple cider

2 ounces tonic water

1 orange wheel, for garnish

Combine the grape juice, syrups, and bitters in a large wineglass over ice. Stir to combine, then top with the sparkling cider and tonic water. Garnish with the orange wheel.

+1 Alcohol: Substitute Campari for the aperitif syrup, as they taste nearly identical and are interchangeable in converting all cocktails and mocktails. An Italian white wine like pinot grigio can sub in for the white grape juice, and prosecco for the sparkling cider.

Overwatch

An online multiplayer hero shooter, this game pits teams of players against each other in matches and missions. Heroes have their distinctive move sets and roles on the team, allowing the development of expertise alongside experimentation. Play as a Damage, Tank, or Support hero and round out the team to win the match. *Overwatch 2*, the currently supported sequel game, is free to play and introduces new player-versus-environment challenges with a deeper story mode: a world ravaged by a near-future robot uprising.

Hanzo Highball

Japanese archer Hanzo Shimada was one of the original twenty-one heroes in 2016's *Overwatch*. A sniper Damage hero, he can also summon a gigantic spirit dragon in battle. His arrows are quiet and hard to see, a compelling asset on the field of battle. This drink is light on its feet and as powerful as the Storm Bow.

YIELD: 1 COCKTAIL

2 ounces Japanese whisky

½ ounce lemon cordial (see page 24)

½ ounce dry vermouth

2 to 4 dashes grapefruit bitters

4 ounces seltzer

Combine the whisky, lemon cordial, vermouth, and bitters in a mixing glass, then add ice. Stir for 15 seconds, until frosty, then strain into a highball glass over fresh ice. Top with the seltzer.

League of Legends

This online multiplayer battle arena game is the largest esport in the world! Teams of five control champions with unique abilities and fighting styles in Summoner's Rift. A combative match with elements of capture the flag, environmental survival, and good old-fashioned fighting, each game is unique with the interplay of team and opponent dynamics. More than 160 champions are available to play, offering fresh challenges and opportunities for newcomers and experienced players alike. Flavor text invites and intrigues, but it's gameplay that counts. Fight on!

Refillable Potion

Inspired by one of the game's health potions, this refreshing punch will restore your good humor with each frosty sip. If your teammates are playing alongside you, you can enjoy the punch together as you rack up each victorious match. If you're all in different time zones, you'll be able to refill your cup all session long. Just remember the effects of the potion are sequential, not stackable.

YIELD: 24 COCKTAILS

1 (750 mL) bottle gin

4 cups iced green tea

2 cups fresh lime juice

1½ cups pineapple juice

1 cup Peach Shrub (page 20)

¾ cup honey syrup (see page 18)

¾ cup St-Germain elderflower liqueur

1 (1 L) bottle lemon-lime soda

Combine the gin, iced tea, juices, shrub, syrup, and liqueur in a punch bowl. Stir to combine and let sit until party time. If the wait will be longer than 4 hours, cover and store in the fridge.

When your first guest arrives, add a large ice ball (see box on page 154) and several large fruit-infused ice cubes (see box on page 33) and top with the lemon-lime soda. Ladle into stemmed cocktail glasses or punch cups.

Hot tip: For extra zing, try adding a dash of orange bitters.

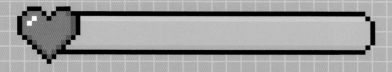

Garnish Game: Large Ice

The easiest way to make ice for punch is to fill a metal bowl three-quarters of the way with water—remember that water expands as it freezes, so don't fill all the way to the top. Be sure to use a metal bowl for this because the thermal shock could crack glass! Store the bowl in the freezer overnight. When it's time to serve your punch, run warm water over the bottom of the bowl or set the bowl in warm water until the ice can be released. Now it is ready to be floated in your punch bowl to keep your drinks refreshingly cool all night long.

Garnish Game: Chocolate Coin

Remove the wrapper from a chocolate coin and place it on a small piece of wax paper. Heat a kitchen knife under hot running water. Cut a slit into the chocolate coin, about halfway through, allowing the chocolate to melt along the surface of the knife. While the chocolate is still soft, slide it onto the rim of your glass.

Fortnite

An online fighting game best known for its battle royale mode where players skydive onto an island and fight to be the sole survivor in an increasingly hostile environment, *Fortnite* is a true cultural phenomenon. Even beyond gameplay, the character emotes have been mimicked by professional athletes and influencers alike, and a vibrant esports community thrives around the game. Beloved by young gamers and seasoned pros, there's always time to try and fight to be the last one standing.

V-Buck

Sometimes it can feel like game developers are out to get your every penny, bringing you back for the coolest items, the fastest speeds. It's nice to get ahead, but those costs can sure add up! Enter the V-Buck, a bittersweet cocktail to wash away the pain in your wallet. Pay to win doesn't feel good, but at least it can taste good. And the enjoyment of this cocktail is more than just cosmetic!

YIELD: 1 COCKTAIL

¾ ounce dark crème de cacao

¾ ounce amaretto

¾ ounce heavy cream

¾ ounce aromatic bitters

1 chocolate coin (see box on page 155), for garnish

Combine the crème de cacao, amaretto, cream, and bitters in a shaker and top with ice. Shake for 15 seconds, until chilled, then strain the liquid into the small tin. Discard the ice and shake for another 15 seconds (reverse dry shake—see box on page 73). Strain into a stemmed cocktail glass and garnish with a chocolate coin.

Loot Box Bridge Mix

Nothing sets a party mood like a bridge mix, an easy munching experience where you never know what you're gonna get. These special treats might arrive via llama in *Fortnite*, but for your cocktail party, a nice bowl will do the trick.

Plan to make about 4 cups of mix with various treats and snacks to enjoy. After all, you don't want to spend your party having to whip up a fresh batch while all your friends are playing.

The adventure is in building a balanced snack mix: something bready like pretzels, something cheesy like Goldfish or Cheez-Its, something nutty like almonds or peanuts, and perhaps something a little sweet like malted milk balls or other chocolate treats (a candy shell is helpful for keeping fingers clean) or dried fruit (like cherries, pineapple, mango, ginger, raisins). Try out different combinations; a little sweet and a little salty reigns supreme when you combine praline pecans (page 82) with dried apricots, pretzel sticks, and chocolate chips. Or bring the heat with some wasabi peas, smoked almonds, corn nuts, and Goldfish crackers. Honey-roasted peanuts, dried cherries, chocolate chips, and potato sticks make for an exciting surprise with every bite. Salted peanuts with candy corn is an autumnal favorite at my parties! (After all, who doesn't love a limited-edition holiday-themed weapon, armor, or cosmetic item?)

The loot box relies on the probability of its prizes: there are common rewards and rare cosmetic items that appear only once in a blue moon. With your bridge mix, you choose the prizes and their ratios. For a really authentic experience, choose a favorite treat (for me, a roasted pecan) and include only one or two in the bowl.

PARTY GAMES

S ome games are just made for multiplayer, for the scrum of jostled shoulders on the couch, for arguments that start with yelling and end with laughter, for bitter rivalries with those you hold dear. And of course, a refreshing beverage. These games need drinks that will play well with your crowd, something you can make early and enjoy through the evening. In this chapter we have punches and batched beverages to keep the drinks flowing and the gameplay lasting well into the night.

Mario Kart

The most popular spinoff series in the Mario franchise, the Mario Kart racing games debuted in 1992 with *Super Mario Kart* for the SNES. With more than a dozen games across half a dozen consoles, there is a Mario Kart for each generation of gamers and racers. Whether you're out at the arcade or chilling at home with your Nintendo Switch, you can always play with friends in person or online, or pit your racing chops against the game's AI opponents. With a bright world of go-kart racetracks, whimsical power-ups, and the lovable cast of characters from across the Mario franchise and beyond, Mario Kart is a premiere party game and enduring staple.

Princess Peach Bellini

Princess Peach is a ruler, damsel, and heroine all in one. First appearing in 1985 in *Super Mario Bros.* with her bright pink dress and blond bouffant, she has grown to become one of the most recognizable characters in the world of video games. Peach holds the crown for more video game appearances than any other female video game character and, in 2020, she was voted the second most popular character in Mario Kart, right behind the eponymous plumber himself. This is a drink as pink and effervescent as the ruler of the Mushroom Kingdom.

YIELD: 1 MOCKTAIL

2 ounces Peach Shrub (page 20)

2 dashes orange bitters

4 ounces sparkling apple cider

1 orange twist (see box on page 79), for garnish

Combine the shrub and bitters in a champagne flute and stir to mix. Top with the sparkling cider and garnish with the orange twist.

Bonus: This may be a bit bright for some tastes, but you can always add a splash of Simple Syrup (page 17) to soften and sweeten the mocktail.

+1 Alcohol: Add 1 ounce brandy and you'll be all set. Or you can replace the sparkling cider with champagne or prosecco.

Super Smash Bros.

A premier fighting game, *Super Smash Bros.* has been bringing together characters from across the world of video games since 1999. The arena is as much a part of the match as the opponent, with the goal of each competition not the depletion of the opponent's health, but rather knocking them out of bounds and off the stage. This makes for a more family-friendly fighting game than *Mortal Kombat* or others, as does the representation of classic Nintendo characters and others from franchises for all ages. Perfect for casual competition and fierce rivalry, *Smash* is the ideal game for a party, but single-player Classic Mode ensures that there's always a way to hone your skills in the arena.

Falcon Punch

Captain Falcon's signature move, this punch is a slow but devastating attack. The air captain is wreathed in flames as he strikes forward toward his opponent. At your next *Smash* tournament, try this spiced and fiery punch for a crowd-pleasing drink that will last all night. For extra authenticity, make sure to yell "Falcon . . . PUNCH!" each time you ladle up a glass.

YIELD: 24 COCKTAILS

1 (750 mL) bottle bourbon whiskey

4 cups apple cider

2 cups fresh lemon juice

½ cup Ginger Syrup (page 21)

½ cup cinnamon syrup (see page 18)

½ cup maple syrup

¼ cup aromatic bitters

1 (2 L) bottle ginger ale

Flaming orange wheels (page 37), for garnish

Combine the bourbon, cider, lemon juice, syrups, and bitters in a punch bowl. Stir and let sit until party time. If the wait will be longer than 4 hours, cover and store in the fridge.

When your first guest arrives, add a large block of ice (see page 154) and top with the ginger ale. Ladle into stemmed cocktail glasses or punch cups. Garnish each cocktail with a flaming orange wheel.

+1 Nonalcoholic: Substitute 3 cups strongly brewed black tea for the bottle of bourbon.

Among Us

Social deduction game *Among Us* debuted in 2018. The game really came to the fore in 2020, when online play allowed for co-op parties with friends and strangers, all housebound by the COVID-19 pandemic lockdown. Crewmates must band together to find the Impostor in their midst, while the Impostor works to kill off each Crewmate one by one. Minigame tasks can be used to weed out the Impostor, but you never know who is faking it. And a variety of maps provide plenty of opportunities for fresh gameplay. Whether you're playing with family and friends or strangers around the world, this game is a rollicking good time for gamers of all ages.

Impostor Shot

A red-pink shot is a much nicer reportable object than a dead body. This drink can be scaled up from four to fifteen players—or even more, as there are no limits at a cocktail party the way there are in the game.

YIELD: 4 SHOTS

1 bar spoon Hot Chili Tincture (page 22)

3 bar spoons Simple Syrup (page 17), divided

3 ounces aged rum

2 ounces Raspberry Liqueur (page 22)

1 ounce cream of coconut

Add the bar spoon of chili tincture to 1 shot glass and 1 bar spoon of simple syrup to the remaining 3 shot glasses. Shuffle the shot glasses. Combine the rum, liqueur, and cream of coconut in a shaker, then add ice. Shake for 15 seconds, until frosty, and strain an equal amount into each shot glass. Can you figure out which of your friends is the Impostor?

Hot tip: To play longer, replace the rum with dry sherry, making a lower ABV version of the base drink.

Dead by Daylight

An asymmetrical survival game for five players, *Dead by Daylight* pits four Survivors against one Killer charged with sacrificing all other players to the Entity. If the Survivors can power up the exit gates, they can escape, but if not, they'll fall to the machinations of the Killer. This game debuted in 2016, and while the game is known for its original characters, they also license characters from the iconic horror-slasher properties like *A Nightmare on Elm Street*. Continuous updates and downloadable content keep the game fresh and exciting—and keep your heart racing.

The Hook

Not for the faint of heart, this drink is sharp and bitter; it will burn and sting but has a touch of sweetness red as blood. Like the weapons of the Killer, it comes with a dark purpose, and many may wish to flee. Those with a sturdy palate who court the darkness will be rewarded with an intense cocktail with a fierce kick.

YIELD: 1 COCKTAIL

1 ounce overproof rum

1 ounce blended Scotch whisky

1 ounce fresh lime juice

½ ounce Grenadine (page 19)

¼ ounce Hot Chili Tincture (page 22)

6 to 8 dashes aromatic bitters

1 fresh hot pepper, for garnish

Combine the rum, Scotch, lime juice, grenadine, chili tincture, and bitters in a shaker, then top with ice. Stir for 20 seconds, then strain into an old-fashioned glass over a single large ice cube. Garnish with a hot pepper hook (see box).

Garnish Game: Hot Pepper Hook

This works best with a cayenne pepper or jalapeño. Cut the stem off the pepper, then slice it down the middle along one side and remove the seeds. Flatten the pepper and cut out a fishhook shape with a paring knife. Don't forget the barb. Make sure your hands are free of capsaicin and then enjoy. Most peppers can yield 2 or 3 garnish hooks.

Fall Guys

A free-to-play online battle royale game, *Fall Guys* pits groups of up to forty against each other in mini-games and obstacle courses, eliminating players round by round until one reigns supreme. Change up your costume for a cute new look and enjoy the changing seasonal theme that keeps gameplay fresh in this relaxing, family-friendly party game.

Marshmallow Man

The eponymous Fall Guys are brightly colored marshmallow-shaped avatars, roly-poly and full of charm. This frosty, frothy mocktail is a sweet treat to enjoy round after round. *Fall Guys* changes through the season, so try swapping the blueberry grenadine for cherry or pomegranate!

YIELD: 1 MOCKTAIL

2 ounces whole milk

¾ ounce blueberry grenadine (see page 19)

½ ounce Orgeat (page 23)

1 bar spoon vanilla extract

1 chocolate-covered marshmallow (see box on page 168), for garnish

Combine the milk, grenadine, orgeat, and vanilla in a shaker, then add ice. Shake for 15 seconds, then strain the liquid back into the small tin. Discard the ice and shake for another 15 seconds (reverse dry shake—see box on page 73). Pour into a stemmed cocktail glass and garnish with the chocolate-covered marshmallow.

Garnish Game: Chocolate-Covered Marshmallows

16 ounces white chocolate chips	¼ cup each of assorted toppings (sprinkles, chopped peanuts, sea salt, etc.)
2 to 4 drops of food coloring	
24 marshmallows	

Line a rimmed baking sheet with wax paper.

Pour an inch or so of water into a small saucepan and bring to a simmer over medium-low heat. Set a heatproof bowl over the simmering water, making sure the bottom of the bowl doesn't touch the water. Put half of the white chocolate chips in the bowl and stir occasionally until fully melted. Add your choice of food coloring and stir to combine. (Remember, as with bitters, it's easy to add more color and hard to add less, so start off slow.) Place a marshmallow on the end of a toothpick and dip it in the melted chocolate, taking care to coat the entire marshmallow. You may wish to roll the chocolate-covered marshmallow in one or more toppings; work quickly to avoid the chocolate setting. Place the marshmallow on the lined baking sheet. Coat half of the marshmallows in the same way. Wash out the bowl and repeat the process with the remaining chocolate chips and a second color food dye to mix and match your marshmallows. Refrigerate until set. Leave the toothpicks in the chocolate-covered marshmallows for easy garnishing.

Tip: If your melted chocolate is too thick to dip your marshmallows, try adding 1 tablespoon coconut oil. The oil is solid at room temperature but melts quickly, so it can add some extra flexibility to your chocolate without compromising the coating of the final treat.

LEVEL COMPLETE

CONTINUE?

Games bring us together. They tell stories, present challenges, and synthesize emotion and action. When we come together for play, we are our best selves. Hosting and making drinks for friends tends the body, while play and competition feed the soul. Whether you're connected to the storytelling experience in a single-player game or locked in fierce combat with friends (and strangers) you hold dear, a good drink is easy to find and makes for a happy evening. From my earliest days playing *Zoombinis*, to spending Christmas break with the *World of Warcraft* free-to-play edition, to the pandemic summer during which I devoured the entire Ace Attorney series, games have been a source of joy in my life—a comfort, a community, a connection. The celebration I find in gaming is the same happiness I find in sitting on the porch with a friend and a drink in hand, or in reading a good book that plays with structure and draws me into its world. I'd like to raise a glass to many years of good drinks and great games to come.

GAME ON!

END CREDITS

To my parents for giving me endless support, for raising me to follow my dreams in words and in recipes, for teaching me to make my own ingredients, and to craft with care. To Aidan and Lillian, you are much better than me at every multiplayer game. To Marissa, *The Oregon Trail* is much better as a drink than adapted to a card game.

To my friends Meredith and Kori, for listening to me in the GC and providing constant encouragement and insight. To Kit, your keen insights on some critical titles are deeply appreciated. To Jason, for bringing me into your Discord for unfamiliar games. My thanks to Nathan for introducing me to Ace Attorney, a major step on the path to this book. To Ben, for listening, for taste-testing, for coordinating photo day by my side. To KP and Bilal, you are simply the best.

To Lonnie, Anthony, and the entire Boston Shaker team, I learned from you, we got through the pandemic arm in arm, and I am proud to sail the ship with you.

My thanks to Saint Gibson, my dear friend and agent. You make all good things happen and I could not ask for a better advocate.

My thanks to Britny Perilli, caretaker, shepherd, editor extraordinaire, a dream to work with, and a true delight. I am so grateful for your faith, for your comments, for making this book the best that it can be. To the team at Running Press, Leah Gordon, Tanvi Baghele, Elizabeth Parks, Seta Zink, and the rest of the marketing and publicity team, for all your hard work, and to Solji Lee, who illustrated this book and brought our drinks to technicolor life.

To the readers, the savvy sippers, the gamers who choose to pick up this book, I hope you find both familiar favorites and new friends.

Thank you.

INDEX